ENVISION ENGLISH

Reading and Writing
for Advanced ESL Learners

GEORGE ELLINGTON

Salt Lake Community College

Kendall Hunt
publishing company

Kendall Hunt
publishing company

www.kendallhunt.com
Send all inquiries to:
4050 Westmark Drive
Dubuque, IA 52004-1840

Copyright © 2014 by Kendall Hunt Publishing Company

ISBN 978-1-4652-3867-2

Printed in the United States of America
10 9 8 7 6 5 4 3 2 1

CONTENTS

ARCHAEOLOGY

The term "archaeology" comes from a Greek word meaning "ancient."
In that case, what is archaeology? What does an archaeologist do?
Look at the images below and discuss the following questions.

1. What are the people in the first image doing? What is the purpose of their work? What tools and methods do they use to achieve this purpose?

2. Does this seem like easy work to you? Does it seem exciting? Boring? Many archaeologists depend on the contributions of students to their work. Would you ever consider joining an excavation like this?

3. Have you ever visited an ancient or archaeological site? Describe the site and your experiences there. Where were you? What did you see? How did it make you feel?

4. The second image illustrates the kinds of artifacts that might be uncovered through archaeology. What value do you think such artifacts have? Is it worthwhile digging them up and displaying them in museums? Or would it be better to just leave the past buried?

ARCHAEOLOGY

A. Here are our target vocabulary for Reading 1 in this unit:

attribute	element	method	research
demonstrate	evidence	persistent	reveal
devote	inevitably	region	transformation

B. Look at the following vocabulary words in context. Can you find synonyms in the text to help you understand the meaning of the highlighted words? Circle the synonyms you find.

1. Today archaeologists are still **devoted** to uncovering the cultures of the past, but they are also committed to respecting those cultures and demonstrating the utmost care in **revealing** artifacts and in preserving the artifacts that they have uncovered.

2. Anger and battle and vengeance—these are the key **elements** to Homer's story. And it was these components that Schliemann was looking for in his excavations at the site of Hıssarlık—**evidence** of death and destruction. Naturally enough, he found it. In a site as old as that of Hıssarlık with as many layers of habitation as it possesses— nine distinct layers covering some three millennia—any archaeologist will inevitably discover signs of death.

C. You may not be able to find a synonym in the text you are reading for words that you do not know. However, you may be able to guess the meaning of the word by taking it apart and looking at the pieces: the prefix, suffix, or root of the word. For example:

reveal → *re + veal = to pull **back** ("re") a **veil** ("veal") [i.e., to let someone see something]*

Look at the following vocabulary words. Write the correct meaning for the highlighted root words from the following choices:

build	*see*	*find*	*select*	*give*
love	*look for*	*use*	*shape*	*want*

1. attribute   →   a(t) + **trib** + ute   =   _____

2. devote   →   de + **vote**   =   _____

3. evidence   →   e + **vid** + ence   =   _____

4. research   →   re + **search**   =   _____

5. transformation   →   trans + **form** + ation   =   _____

D. Choose from the vocabulary words to complete the passage below.

attribute	*element*	*method*	*research*
demonstrate	*evidence*	*persistent*	*reveal*
devote	*inevitably*	*region*	*transformation*

When Carol Wingate visited a used bookstore recently, she was not expecting to make an amazing

discovery, but that is exactly what she did. She was leafing through a large old travel book about the

_____ **(a)** of Vienna in Austria. When she flipped through the pages, she

_____ **(b)** a hidden manuscript, uncovering a sheet of music written by hand and

apparently very old. She took the manuscript to a friend of hers who is

deeply _____ **(c)** to music, spending all of his free

time playing different instruments. Her friend said he could not be sure, but

that there was _____ **(d)** in the manuscript to

indicate that this music may have been written by a well-known composer.

To be certain, he took the music to Professor Louis Montaigne at the

university, an expert who conducts _____ **(e)** on

classical music. After careful examination, Professor Montaigne felt

confident enough to _____ **(f)** the work to none

other than Wolfgang Amadeus Mozart himself!

E. Write the letter of the word in each list that best completes the sentence.

1. After she failed to find any answers, Melissa's teacher suggested
    that she use a different _____ in her research.

    a. method

    b. methodical

2. I am confident that Carlos will complete his project without errors.
    He is very _____ in his work.

    c. methodically

    d. methodism

3. If you _____ follow the plan for our project, you will
    achieve more accurate results.

    e. methodology

---

4. The Church has a long history of using _____ music, such as
    hymns that accompany religious rituals.

    f. devote

    g. devoted

5. You cannot question Xin's _____ to her children. She would
    do anything she could to take care of them.

    h. devotee

    i. devotion

6. Cheryl enjoys most music, but she is a true _____ of jazz.
    She attends every jazz concert that comes to town.

    j. devotional

3

ARCHAEOLOGY

Active reading can help you better understand a college text. Begin by discussing the questions below. Then carefully read the essay "Dreams of Troy," taking notes on the main points and important details that you find in the text. Also select the best meaning for words highlighted in the right-hand column.

Heinrich Schliemann

PREREADING DISCUSSION

1. Have you ever heard of Heinrich Schliemann? What can you tell about him?
2. What kind of training do you think an archaeologist should have?
3. What should archaeologists do with the artifacts that they find?
4. What do you know about the story of the Trojan War? Who wrote it?
5. The hero of the story is a warrior named Achilles. What are the qualities or abilities of a hero?

(1)   The early years of archaeology may strike one as involving more of the elements of tomb raiders and grave robbers than of professional archaeologists. Sad to say, this was often the case. As with all new fields, the profession of archaeology had to undergo a painful period of growth and transformation as new
5   theories were considered and new methods tested in the field. Today archaeologists are still devoted to uncovering the cultures of the past, but they are also committed to respecting those cultures and demonstrating the utmost care in revealing artifacts and in preserving those artifacts that they have uncovered.

(2)   Unfortunately, for some ancient cultures, brutally laid bare by the crude
10   methods of early diggers, the damage has already been done and may never really be undone. Such was the case at the famous city of Troy, located in what is today the western region of Turkey. Long before it was excavated, the city of Troy had existed only in the tales attributed to Homer[1] and in the minds, the imaginations of those familiar with Homer's stories. Chances are you too have
15   heard of the city of Troy. Even if you have not read or heard Homer's stories, you might have been exposed to the name of Troy in a schoolroom or seen one of the many movies made about the Trojan War and the great hero Achilles.

(3)   Had it not been for the persistent ambitions of one man in particular, Troy might forever have remained just
20   that—a story. However, for Heinrich Schliemann, Troy was much more than an ancient tale told around a campfire. Schliemann (1822–1890) was born in the village of Neu Buckow in Germany to Ernst and Luise Schliemann. As a boy, Schliemann was exposed to the tales of Homer—to the
25   greed of Agamemnon, the fury of Achilles, the fall of Troy— and his passions were inflamed. However, his family's poverty prohibited him from acquiring a university education. Consequently, the adult Schliemann entered the field of archaeology for which he had received no professional
30   training. Nonetheless, with only his dreams and ambitions— and a remarkable capacity for learning languages—to guide him, Schliemann was devoted to finding the real Troy.

(4)   Schliemann began excavations at Hıssarlık in western Turkey in 1870. Popular thinking attributes the discovery of Troy to Schliemann, guided by his
35   inspired readings of Homer's tales. However, this distinction really belonged to

Statue of Achilles from Corfu

---

line 1: strike

a.   *to hit*
b.   *to protest*
c.   *to impress*

Another example:
You failed the first and second test. It strikes me that you are not studying enough.

---

yet another amateur archaeologist by the name of Frank Calvert. Schliemann had dug a sounding or test pit at the hill of Pınarbaşı on the Trojan plain, a site previously excavated by the Englishman Calvert, but found nothing of interest. Subsequently, Calvert suggested that he dig at Hıssarlık instead, which Calvert
40   believed to be the true site of Troy. And Calvert was right.

(5)   According to Homer, the city of Troy, known in Greek as *Ilion* or *Ilium*, was the site of a tragic battle. Sometime around the thirteenth century BC, the ruler of Mycenae—King Agamemnon—commanded his subjects to prepare a fleet that would cross the Aegean Sea to besiege the Trojans. The king of Troy,
45   Priam, would be killed. His people would be slaughtered or enslaved. And all for … love? So the ancients would have us believe.

The ruins of Troy

(6)   The story goes that before the Greeks destroyed Troy, the gods had called upon Paris of Troy to judge a competition. Which of the central
50   Greek goddesses was the loveliest: Hera, Athena, or Aphrodite? Each of these powerful goddesses offered Paris a remarkable gift to declare that she was the fairest of all. But Paris was seduced by the gift of Aphrodite, for she—the goddess of love—
55   offered Paris the most beautiful woman in the world as his prize: Helen, Queen of Sparta, wife of King Menelaus. In response to this offer, Paris indeed declared Aphrodite to be the most beautiful goddess. Quickly claiming Helen for himself, Paris
60   stole her away to Troy. King Menelaus of Sparta was understandably enraged at the abduction of his wife. He called upon his brother, King Agamemnon, to help him. And so began one of the most famous battles in history. Or at least in literature.

65   (7)   Yet it was not this tale of desire and betrayal that was at the heart of the story of Homer, which had so deeply inspired Heinrich Schliemann. Homer's epic tale of the *Iliad*—the fall of Ilium—written centuries after the actual battle had taken place, opens with the following declaration:

> *An angry man—there is my story: the bitter rancour of Achilles, prince*
70   > *of the house of Peleus, which brought a thousand troubles upon the*
> *Achaian host. Many a strong soul did it send down to Hades, and left the*
> *heroes themselves a prey to dogs and carrion birds, while the will of God*
> *moved on to fulfillment.[2]*

(8)   Anger and battle and vengeance—these are the key elements to Homer's
75   story. And it was these components that Schliemann was looking for in his excavations at the site of Hıssarlık—evidence of death and destruction. Naturally enough, he found it. In a site as old as that of Hıssarlık with as many layers of habitation as it possesses—nine distinct layers covering some three millennia— any archaeologist will inevitably discover signs of death. However, Schliemann
80   wanted evidence of one layer alone—the city of Priam. He assumed this to be deep down in the hill, and so he dug a trench through multiple layers of habitation, destroying innumerable artifacts, to reach the remnants of a burnt city

---

line 37: sound

a.   noise
b.   experiment
c.   healthy

Another example:
Our sounding well at the property revealed there was just not enough underground water.

---

line 68: take place

a.   to happen
b.   to capture
c.   to move to

Another example:
The first US presidential election took place in 1788-1789.

5

in what is known as Troy II—the second layer. However, he was wrong about Troy II, as he was wrong about so many things.

85 (9)   Research has revealed that the city of Priam was higher up in the hill in Troy VII, a layer of habitation that also includes much evidence of destruction, although Schliemann was always eager to attribute artifacts from
90 any layer of Hıssarlık to Homer's Troy. At one point, for instance, he discovered a small collection of valuable artifacts along with a small key, and he wrote:

95 *It is probably that some member of the family of King Priam hurriedly packed the Treasure into the chest and carried it off without having time to pull out the key; that when he reached the wall, however, the hand*
100 *of an enemy or the fire overtook him, and he was obliged to abandon the chest...[3]*

The remains of Schliemann's trench at Troy

(10)   Schliemann was also eager to describe in his writings his distrust of others, particularly of his workers, whom he assumed were trying to steal from
105 him. He was less eager to acknowledge how persistent he was in his own efforts to steal away these historical artifacts, smuggling them out of Turkey without permission from the Turkish government. Nor does he seem to have felt any guilt over his hasty and quite unprofessional methods, and the loss to the archaeological record that resulted from them.

110 (11)   Finally, Schliemann was not above fabricating tales of his work and life to present himself in a more romantic light to his readers. Years before he excavated Troy, Schliemann had written his supposedly eyewitness account of the 1851 fire of San Francisco, which had taken place while Schliemann was in Sacramento. Likewise, he later wrote about the discovery of the "Treasure" of
115 Troy, and how he immediately ordered his workers to take a break so that he could have exclusive access to the artifacts:

While the men were eating and resting, I cut out the Treasure with a large knife, which it was impossible to do without the very greatest exertion and the most fearful risk of my life, for the great fortification-
120 *wall...threatened every moment to fall down upon me. But the sight of so many objects, every one of which is of inestimable value to archaeology, made me foolhardy, and I never thought of any danger. It would, however, have been impossible for me to have removed the Treasure without the help of my dear wife, who stood by me ready to pack the*
125 *things which I cut out in her shawl and to carry them away.[4]*

Schliemann later admitted that he had lied about this—that his wife Sophia had not been with him at that time. One has to wonder, beyond the excitement of the discovery of Troy, how many more lies have corrupted the revelations of the ancient past of this most famous of cities.

---

line 100: overtake

a. to pass
b. to capture
c. to happen

Another example:
Police overtook the fleeing suspect just outside the college.

---

line 111: romantic

a. loving
b. tender
c. idealistic

Another example:
Hollywood movies present audiences with a too romantic image of violence and killing.

ARCHAEOLOGY

A. Quickly scan through the essay and find two names for each of the following categories.

1. Archaeologists   **a.** _____   **b.** _____

2. Greek goddesses   **a.** _____   **b.** _____

3. Ancient cities   **a.** _____   **b.** _____

4. Royal characters   **a.** _____   **b.** _____

5. Archaeological sites   a. _____   **b.** _____

6. Countries   **a.** _____   **b.** _____

B. Read the following statements. Do they agree with the information in the essay? Circle T (true) or F (false) for each statement.

1.   T   F   Early excavators sometimes seemed more like thieves stealing from the dead than archaeologists uncovering the past.

2.   T   F   Schliemann learned his archaeological methods during his university education.

3.   T   F   Schliemann began searching for the city of Troy at Hıssarlık in Greece.

4.   T   F   Schliemann was the first digger to discover the site of Hıssarlık and to come to the conclusion that this was the site of ancient Troy.

5.   T   F   Schliemann learned about the tales of Troy from the ancient storyteller Homer.

6.   T   F   Homer's story of the fall of Troy, known as *The Iliad*, focuses on Aphrodite and the love of Paris for the beautiful Helen of Sparta.

7.   T   F   Schliemann found five layers of habitation at Hıssarlık and believed Troy VII to be the ancient city described by Homer.

8.   T   F   Schliemann often tried to attribute artifacts discovered at Hıssarlık with objects described in Homer's story.

9.   T   F   Schliemann was careful to gain official permission for every artifact he removed from Turkey.

10.   T   F   Schliemann lied about his wife helping him to steal artifacts inside her shawl.

A statue of Aphrodite excavated at Hıssarlık

C. *Which of the following statements best expresses the thesis or main idea of the essay "Dreams of Troy"? Circle the number of the correct answer.*

1. Many of the early archaeologists damaged the sites they excavated by using crude methods intended to produce quick and profitable results.

2. Although he used crude archaeological methods, Heinrich Schliemann was driven by his passionate interest in an ancient tale to find and uncover the city of Troy.

3. The city of Troy was the site of an epic and heroic battle between the Trojans and the Greeks, a battle incited by the desire for love and revenge.

D. *Academic texts are often composed by more than one writer and are likely to include information and quotations from a large number of sources. As a college reader, you need to be able to distinguish between the different sources of information in a text. And as a college writer, you too may be expected to compose essays that include not only your own ideas, but information from other sources. The essay "Dreams of Troy" includes writing from*

   (1) The author of the essay
   (2) Homer's *The Iliad*
   (3) Schliemann as quoted in *Hands on the Past*, edited by Ceram
   (4) Schliemann as quoted in *Great Adventures in Archaeology*, written by Silverberg

Number each of the following quotes from the text 1, 2, 3, or 4 to indicate their source.

1. _____ Long before it was excavated, the city of Troy had existed only in the tales attributed to Homer and in the minds, the imaginations of those familiar with Homer's stories. *(lines 10–12)*

2. _____ But the sight of so many objects, every one of which is of inestimable value to archaeology, made me foolhardy, and I never thought of any danger. *(lines 118–120)*

3. _____ Many a strong soul did it send down to Hades, and left the heroes themselves a prey to dogs and carrion birds, while the will of God moved on to fulfillment. *(lines 69–71)*

4. _____ In a site as old as that of Hıssarlık with as many layers of habitation as it possesses—nine distinct layers covering some three millennia—any archaeologist will inevitably discover signs of death. *(lines 75–77)*

5. _____ Schliemann had dug a sounding or test pit at the hill of Pınarbaşı on the Trojan plain, a site previously excavated by the Englishman Calvert, but found nothing of interest. *(lines 34–36)*

6. _____ It is probably that some member of the family of King Priam hurriedly packed the Treasure into the chest and carried it off without having time to pull out the key... *(lines 92–96)*

7. _____ In response to this offer, Paris indeed declared Aphrodite to be the most beautiful goddess. *(lines 55–57)*

8. _____ An angry man—there is my story: the bitter rancour of Achilles, prince of the house of Peleus, which brought a thousand troubles upon the Achaian host. *(lines 67–69)*

9. _____ ...when he reached the wall, however, the hand of an enemy or the fire overtook him, and he was obliged to abandon the chest... *(lines 96–100)*

ARCHAEOLOGY

A. THE STRUCTURE AND MEANING OF THE PAST PERFECT TENSE

Look at the following sentences. How are they structurally different from one another?

> I saw that movie.
>
> I had seen that movie.

Is there any difference in meaning between the two sentences above? Can you explain the difference? How about if we change the second sentence? Now try to explain the difference in meaning.

> I saw that movie.
>
> Tim suggested we watch *Iron Man*, but I had seen that movie.

The Simple Past Tense and Past Perfect Tense both describe something that happened in the past—before now. However, we only use the Past Perfect Tense to describe what happened before something else that happened in the past, something that is often described using the Simple Past Tense.

If you describe something in the past, but you also want to describe something before that past event, then you can use the Past Perfect Tense. In that case, the Past Perfect tells you what happened first, while the Simple Past tells you what happened second. In the sentence, you might see the Simple Past event first, but in real time, it is the Past Perfect event that happens first, followed by the Simple Past.

In our example sentence, circle what happened first and underline what happened second.

> Tim suggested we watch *Iron Man*, but I had seen that movie.

B. Do the same thing with these sentences from our reading—circle what happened first and underline what happened second.

1. Long before it was excavated, the city of Troy had existed only in the tales attributed to Homer and in the minds, the imaginations of those familiar with Homer's stories. *(lines 12–14)*

2. Consequently, the adult Schliemann entered the field of archaeology for which he had received no professional training. *(lines 28–30)*

3. The story goes that before the Greeks destroyed Troy, the gods had called upon Paris of Troy to judge a competition. *(lines 49–51)*

4. Years before he excavated Troy, Schliemann had written his supposedly eyewitness account of the 1851 fire of San Francisco, which had taken place while Schliemann was in Sacramento. *(lines 112–15)*

5. Schliemann later admitted that he had lied about this—that his wife Sophia had not been with him at that time. *(lines 127–28)*

C. *Complete the following text by writing the verbs in parentheses in either the Simple Past or Past Perfect Tense.*

Surely one of the greatest finds in archaeological history was the discovery of the tomb of Pharaoh Tut-ankh-Amun and its excavation by Howard Carter. Before traveling to Egypt in 1891, Carter _____ (**1:** *grow up*) in England, where his father, Samuel Carter, _____ (**2:** *train*) Howard in the arts of drawing and painting. Although Howard Carter had no interest in painting the portraits of wealthy landowners in England, it was his artistic skills that enabled Carter to travel to Egypt. After the British Museum had hired Carter to sketch Egyptian tombs, they _____ (**3:** *send*) him to work on the tomb of an Egyptian prince.

He _____ (**4:** *be*) in Egypt less than a year when he was asked to work with Egyptologist Flinders Petrie in 1892. Petrie _____ (**5:** *begin*) his own work in Egypt back in 1880 and _____ (**6:** *excavate*) the lost city of Tanis in 1884. Strangely enough, Petrie did not think Carter would ever become a good archaeologist. He _____ (**7:** *never meet*) Carter before and had no idea what the young Howard Carter was capable of.

Carter, however, had already decided to dedicate himself to the study of ancient Egypt and he _____ (**8:** *be*) determined to prove that he was indeed a skilled and capable researcher. While Petrie _____ (**9:** *have*) his doubts about Carter in 1892, in 1899 Gaston Maspero, the Director of the Egyptian Antiquities Service, _____ (**10:** *offer*) Carter a very high position in Egyptian archaeology, a step in the right direction for the man who would eventually discover King Tut.

D. *Complete the following sentences with your own ideas. Make sure to use the appropriate Past Perfect Tense form of the verbs.*

1. I came to the United States in _____. Before that, I _____
   _____

2. By the time I began to study English, I _____
   _____

3. After I _____, I
   wanted to _____

4. Before I began my first job, I _____
   _____

ARCHAEOLOGY   JOURNAL WRITING 1.1

Choose from the following options for your journal writing assignment:

1. The dream of Heinrich Schliemann was to discover and excavate the once legendary city of Troy, site of the great battle described by Homer. His dream inspired him to learn new languages, to travel the world, and even to take risks with his life. Dreams can inspire us to study, to work, to travel, to explore—to do many things. What dreams do you have? Write about a dream that has inspired you, an aspiration you have had to do something special with your life. How have you pursued that dream? And if you have not followed your dream, why not?

2. Characters such as King Agamemnon or the warrior Achilles are more than just fictional figures in a fantastic story; they become heroes. When Alexander the Great himself crossed the water from Greece to Turkey to begin his conquests, he made his army wait while he looked for the tomb of Achilles so that he, Alexander, could honor the great hero of Troy. How would you define the word "hero?" What are the qualities or abilities of a hero, in your opinion? Is there a particular way that people in your home culture define what it means to be a hero? Have you ever had a hero of your own, someone you deeply admire and wish to emulate? Begin by writing a list of people—real or fictional—whom you admire and perhaps wish to emulate. Then write a journal entry about that hero and how they have inspired you.

3. The story of Troy belongs to a long and very colorful collection of myths that stem from Greek civilization. In ancient Greece, people worshipped many gods and they told and retold stories about those gods and the heroes of old. Such stories are not just entertaining; they often teach people important lessons about life and worship and society and the challenges we face as human beings. Can you think of any stories like that? Perhaps from your own culture? Write a story you are familiar with about heroes or gods. At the end of the story, describe the lesson that you think people are supposed to learn from that story.

Statue of the Greek god Dionysus from the palace of Herrenchiemsee, Germany

ARCHAEOLOGY

A. *Here are our target vocabulary for Reading 2 in this unit:*

accumulation	contribution	duration	indicate
conduct	crucial	ensure	so-called
considerable	document	illustrate	symbolic

B. *If you understand the meaning of prefixes, you can more easily guess the meaning of new words. For example, the prefix "com-" or "con-" derives from Latin and means "with." This is a very common prefix added to many root words to change their meaning. [While suffixes usually change the form of a word, prefixes usually change their meaning.] For example:*

> *confirm → con + firm = with firmness, with certainty, to agree or make something certain*

The original meaning of some academic words may be quite different from the modern meaning, but knowing these original meanings might help you to remember new words. For example:

> *companion → com + pan + ion = with ("com") + bread ("pan") + (noun suffix "ion")*

"With bread?" A "companion" is someone "with bread?" Well, think of it this way—we usually eat with friends, not enemies. We eat with people we like and trust. A "companion" is someone you trust, someone you might travel with or eat with. To illustrate the word "companion," I might say, "When Kim and I became really good friends, we began to spend more time going out to restaurants and cafes. Kim was a very good companion."

Choose five of the following words and write your own sentences to illustrate their meaning.

a.	commission *(with a mission)*	**f.**	conduct *(with leading)*
b.	community *(with unity)*	**g.**	confine *(with limits)*
c.	complain *(with sadness)*	**h.**	considerable *(with size)*
d.	complex *(with twining)*	**i.**	contemplate *(with a temple)*
e.	component *(with putting together)*	**j.**	contribution *(with giving)*

1. _____

   _____

2. _____

   _____

3. _____

   _____

4. _____

   _____

5. _____

   _____

C. *Complete the following text by circling the correct form of each word.*

When someone asks you how you're doing, how much of your answer depends on your financial stability? Let's be honest, just about everyone is in debt, and the amount of money you owe to businesses and banks can put a serious dent in your happiness. The **(1)** *accumulate / accumulative / accumulation* of debt is an increasingly common phenomenon around the world. If you have a credit card, chances are you will use it. And research suggests that the average American has not just one, but three active credit cards. When people have that much credit, they tend not to **(2)** *conduct / conductor / conducive* themselves with great caution when they go shopping. If the high number of bankruptcies in the US is any **(3)** *indicate / indicative / indication*, then high amounts of credit mean that caution goes out the window! The credit card—and the opportunity it provides to shop until you drop—has become a **(4)** *symbol / symbolic / symbolism* of American freedom. To **(5)**

illustrate / illustration / illustrator my point, I'd like you to consider the case of Mary. Mary, you could say, is an average American. She believed that a college education was **(6)** *crucially / crucial / cruciality* for her to get a good job. However, to **(7)** *ensuring / ensures / ensure* that she could attend college, she had to take out loans. By the time she got her first credit card, she was already in debt. Because she was going to school and did not have time for a full-time job, she got a second credit card to pay the bills. By the time she had obtained her third card, she knew it was too late. It will now take Mary **(8)** *considerable / considerably / consideration* longer to pay off her debts than she had predicted. Each card **(9)** *contributed / contributor / contribution* to her future misery. So the next time you ask somebody how they are doing, and they tell you, "Not so good," perhaps you should not ask them a follow-up question about their health. Chances are, they are just suffering through a very **(10)** *durable / duration / endure* Credit Card Syndrome.

D. *For each of the following vocabulary words, there are two synonyms and one antonym. Circle the antonym.*

1.	**considerable**	meager	plentiful	abundant
2.	**contribution**	assistance	helping	hindering
3.	**crucial**	critical	insignificant	necessary
4.	**ensure**	neglect	guarantee	make certain
5.	**indicate**	signify	conceal	demonstrate

ARCHAEOLOGY

Active reading can help you better understand a college text. Begin by discussing the questions below. Then carefully read the essay "Mystery of the Maya," taking notes on the main points and important details that you find in the text. Also select the best meaning for words highlighted in the right-hand column.

PREREADING DISCUSSION

1. Who were the Maya? Where did they live?
2. What kind of cultures existed in the Americas before the Europeans arrived in 1492?
3. How were those American cultures different from European cultures?
4. What kind of monuments were Native American civilizations able to build?
5. How did these ancient peoples conceive of time? Religion? Government?

(1)   In the nineteenth century, the mysterious writing system of ancient Egypt, known as hieroglyphics, was finally deciphered by a brilliant French linguist named Jean François Champollion. Suddenly, the immense history of the Egyptians was open to researchers—some 3,000 years of Egyptian records!

5   However, the Egyptians were not the only ancient people to leave behind a seemingly indecipherable script. There are still documents today that cannot be read, because their codes have not yet been broken, including the pre-Greek Linear A script of the Minoans and the Harappan writing system of ancient India. The script of the Maya in Mexico and Central America was just such an

10   enigma to researchers for many years, until the extraordinary efforts of talented archaeologists and linguists at last decoded the mystery of the Maya.

A hieroglyphic inscription from ancient Egypt

(2)   The history of excavations of the ancient Maya began with events and characters just as colorful as those in Sumeria, Babylonia, and Egypt. In this case, it began in the autumn of 1839, when John Lloyd Stephens (1805–1852)

15   and illustrator Frederick Catherwood (1799–1854) were shown the ruins of Copan in Honduras, a site covered by the ever encroaching forest. Stephens was born in 1805 in New Jersey and grew up in New York City. He had been trained in law, but a legal career held little appeal for Stephens, who was a romantic at heart and longed to see the world. Stephens was in fact a traveler, an aspiration

20   he sought to finance by writing books about his journeys.

line 7: break
a. to smash
b. to decipher
c. to violate
Another example:
Agents worked through the night trying to break the secret code.

(3)   Stephens' first two travel books were quite positively received, but he still longed to see and do more with his life. While in the Holy Land, Stephens relied on a map drawn by a man named Frederick Catherwood. Stephens was so impressed by the map that he decided to seek out Catherwood in London and

25   invite him along on his further adventures. Catherwood showed Stephens a letter written by a Colonel Galindo that described his visit to the ancient ruins of the Mayan site of Palenque in Mexico. The two men decided to go and see the Yucatan for themselves, with Stephens planning to write up the accounts of their journeys, while Catherwood would illustrate the books.

line 22: long
a. lengthy
b. boring
c. desire
Another example:
Manuel longs to return to his native Spain.

30   (4)   Stephens and his companion left for Central America in October 1839. Despite the dangers of traveling through the region at that time, the two men returned in 1841, making their way back to Copan. For 10 months they explored the ruins of this ancient Mayan city, trying to reconstruct what the site must have looked like. They had to cope with the suspicion of the locals (who were dubious

35   of these outsiders) and of local governors (who were outright hostile), not to mention the suffering they endured in such an uncomfortable and mosquito-

infested environment. Yet the greatest obstacle to his work at Copan, Stephens understood, would be his lack of legal rights over the ruins, which stood on land leased to a local farmer, who could at any time demand that Stephens leave and
40   never return. The story is that Stephens did something that archaeologists today generally have neither the opportunity nor the funds to accomplish. John Lloyd Stephens supposedly bought Copan, acquired for the fantastic sum of $50! In truth, he only purchased the right to map and explore the site.

(5)   One of the first things that Stephens and Catherwood noticed about
45   Copan was an immense wall, which Stephens estimated to be 100 feet high, but which we now know was not a wall at all, but the hillside of the city. Within this so-called wall, archaeologists have found the remains of over 2,000 years of habitation, indicating that each successive ruler tended to build upon the remains of his predecessors. Stephens was astonished by the majesty of such structures:

50   *We sat down on the very edge of the wall, and strove in vain to penetrate the mystery by which we were surrounded. Who were the people that built this city? In the ruined cities of Egypt, even in long-lost Petra, the stranger knows the story of the people whose vestiges are around him. America, say historians, was peopled by savages; but savages never*
55   *reared these structures, savages never carved these stones. We asked the Indians who made them, and their dull answer was "Quien sabe?" "who knows?"* [5]

(6)   In the following months, Stephens directed his native workers from one structure to the next, ordering them to clear the building or altar or stela of
60   the undergrowth that had covered it over. Catherwood would then follow in their wake and produce illustrated manuscripts of the newly uncovered monuments. Catherwood and Stephens were understandably fascinated with the many stelae discovered at Copan. Some are located in and outside the city, while a special cluster stand in the Grand Plaza, placed there on the orders of
65   King 18 Rabbit, who is depicted in Stelae A, B, and H. Each stela honored a particular lord of Copan, one of the 16 or 17 generations of kings who ruled the great city in the name of the god of the sun, the chief deity of the Maya.

(7)   As semi-divine rulers, the kings of Copan were typically depicted in flawless form, symbolic of their perfection. And they carried symbols as well.
70   In Stela B we see King 18 Rabbit holding one of the most important of the royal scepters—the double-headed ceremonial bar, a symbol of the highest religious rank among the Maya. You also see other symbols associated with kingship. Just as Egyptian pharaohs and Assyrian kings were typically portrayed with a beard, a symbol of royalty, so too the rulers of Copan were
75   bearded. King 18 Rabbit is shown with a shell beard hanging from his cheeks. The people were also meant to understand from this stela that their lord exercised the power of life and death over them. In Stela B, King 18 Rabbit is portrayed as the god Chac, the executioner wielding an ax.

(8)   The story of the stelae was not only displayed in the images, but detailed
80   in the inscriptions that accompanied each figure. These hieroglyphic inscriptions covered the back and sides of the stelae, beckoning the researcher to read about the Mayan past. However, for centuries no one could do so, including Stephens and Catherwood. They helped inspire the imaginations of others to explore the Mayan civilization, yet they could not read the documents composed by the

Stela B from Copan depicting King 18 Rabbit as the executioner god Chac

---

line 37: greatest

a.   largest
b.   highest
c.   best

Another example:
The greatest problem we now face is finding more money to fund our excavation.

---

line 48: tend

a.   to be likely
b.   to take care of
c.   to nurse

Another example:
Leon tends to get up very early every morning and to go to bed quite late.

---

85   Maya. For that to happen, Mayan hieroglyphics required another Jean François Champollion, you might say. As Stephens himself wrote,

> *In regard to the age of this desolate city I shall not at present offer any*
> *conjecture. Some idea might perhaps be formed from the accumulations of earth*
> *and the gigantic trees growing on the top of the ruined structures, but it would be*
90 > *uncertain and unsatisfactory. Nor shall I at this moment offer any conjecture in*
> *regard to the people who built it, or to the time when or the means by which it*
> *was depopulated, and became a desolation and ruin... One thing I believe, that*
> *its history is graven on its monuments. No Champollion has yet brought to them*
> *the energies of his inquiring mind. Who shall read them?* [6]

95   **(9)**   A man who spent a great deal of time attempting to decipher Mayan hieroglyphics was Sir John Eric Sidney Thompson (1898–1975). Thompson was born in London and studied anthropology at the University of Cambridge. He spent considerable time examining Mayan ceramics, art, iconography, archaeology, and even ethnology.
100   Nonetheless, it was his expertise in the Mayan script, particularly as it related to the distinct Mayan calendars, that allowed Thompson to make such a valuable contribution to our understanding of pre-Columbian Mayan civilization.

An extensive hieroglyphic inscription on the back of a stela at Copan

(10)   As the Mayan population grew, the need for more food
105   became crucial. This need was fulfilled by farmers selecting different corn varieties and carefully coordinating the dates of cultivation with the rain cycle. The need to properly understand and prepare for the planting and harvesting seasons led to the development of a solar calendar, the *haab*, which was made up of 18 months of 20 days each,
110   which comes out to 360 days. At the end of the year was a five-day month known as the *wayeb*. These were dangerous or unlucky days, nameless days when the boundary between this realm and the realm of the spirits dissolved. To ensure the safety of the living against the threats from the spirits, the Maya performed various rituals and
115   conducted themselves in peculiar ways during these five days.

(11)   The Maya also employed a different calendar for ceremonial purposes, a calendar that was sensitive to the rhythms of the earth and the necessity of pleasing the gods and performing the proper rituals at just the right time. Yet even this calendar was influenced by agricultural observations. This was the
120   *tzolkin* or ceremonial calendar. The time count consisted of the number of fingers on both hands and toes on both feet or the number 20, known as a *kal*. The 13 *kal* (a duration of 260 days) involved in selecting the fields, preparing the soil, planting the corn seeds, nurturing their growth, and harvesting the crops may have given rise to the *tzolkin* calendar.[7]

125   **(12)**   Such an interest in time took into account not only beginnings but endings. The Maya believed that the gods had attempted three failed creations before accomplishing the fourth and successful creation, the one that included humankind. However, the fourth creation too must come to an end. An inscription at the ancient Mayan city of Palenque records that this fourth created
130   world will come to an end in a terrible catastrophe, although not for some time—perhaps on 13 October 4772. At that time, a fifth and final creation will take place, signaling the end of mankind.

---

line 116: employ

a.   to hire
b.   to keep busy
c.   to use

Another example:
Schliemann employed the most primitive methods of excavation.

ARCHAEOLOGY

READING COMPREHENSION
MYSTERY OF THE MAYA

A. *Quickly scan for the following information from the text. (All of the answers involve numbers.)*

1. How many days are there in the Mayan *tzolkin* calendar? _____

2. In which year did Stephens and Catherwood first travel to Central America? _____

3. In which year was John Stephens born? _____

4. How many days were in the Mayan *haab* calendar? _____

5. In which year did John Thompson die? _____

6. How much did John Stephens pay to explore Copan? _____

7. In which year did Stephens and Catherwood begin to excavate Copan? _____

8. According to the Maya, in which year will this world end? _____

9. How long did Stephens and Catherwood study Copan? _____

10. How many years have people lived at Copan? _____

B. *Answer the following questions about the text.*

1. What comparison does the writer make between the Egyptian and Mayan civilizations? _____
   _____

2. What ancient script was deciphered by Champollion? _____

3. What profession did John Stephens reject? _____

4. Why did Stephens want to meet Catherwood? _____
   _____

5. Write three obstacles Stephens faced in his work at Copan. _____
   _____
   _____

6. Which god was the chief deity of the Maya? _____

7. Write two common aspects of the kings in the stelae of Copan. _____
   _____
   _____

8. What does the writer suggest was John Thompson's greatest contribution to our understanding of
   the Maya? _____

9. Describe two of the Mayan calendars and their purposes. _____
   _____
   _____

C. *Academic essays are typically written in an order and follow a pattern of organization that allows the reader to understand more easily what the writer is saying: to learn the information the writer has shared or to follow the argument that the writer has made. A logical order in your own writing should make your compositions clearer and more effective. Below are fifteen main ideas. Twelve of these main ideas match the twelve paragraphs of the essay "Mystery of the Maya." Write the number of the paragraph next to the appropriate main idea. Write an "X" next to the three remaining main ideas.*

a. _____ Agricultural needs also influenced the development of the *tzolkin* calendar, a calendar associated with rituals dedicated to the Mayan gods.

b. _____ John Lloyd Stephens, a writer and traveler, and illustrator Frederick Catherwood first saw the site of Copan, Honduras in 1839.

c. _____ Mayan calendars even predicted the end of this fourth creation of the world, which is expected to be destroyed by a great disaster in the year 4772.

d. _____ Stephens oversaw the clearing of the site while Catherwood made his illustrations, particularly of the many stelae at Copan.

e. _____ Mayan hieroglyphics was one of several ancient scripts that could not be deciphered, much like the Linear A script of the Minoans or the Harappan system of India.

f. _____ Stephens was amazed by the magnificence of the structures at Copan and wondered at the mystery of whom the Maya had been.

g. _____ Stephens entered a law school in Connecticut after graduating from Columbia College at the age of 18.

h. _____ The stelae of Copan, along with their symbols, portray the perfection and vast power of the ancient Mayan kings.

i. _____ Stephens was convinced that the history of the Maya was written in the hieroglyphic symbols along the stelae of Copan, but no one could read them.

j. _____ The cultivation of corn was essential to the growing Mayan civilization, and to assist farmers, the Maya developed a 365-day calendar known as a *haab*.

k. _____ Impressed by the drawings of Catherwood, Stephens invited the illustrator to join him for an exploration of the Yucatan in Mexico.

l. _____ Stephens and Catherwood visited forty-four ancient sites in all, including the incredible Mayan city of Palenque in Mexico.

m. _____ With his expertise in the Mayan script, John Eric Sidney Thompson made a valuable contribution to our understanding of Mayan history and culture.

n. _____ Stephens and Catherwood returned to Copan in 1841 to further explore the site, although they encountered a number of obstacles to their work.

o. _____ Catherwood was an architect and illustrator who made detailed drawings of ancient sites in Egypt, Greece, and Turkey.

ARCHAEOLOGY

A. THE STRUCTURE AND MEANING OF REDUCED RELATIVE CLAUSES

Relative clauses help to describe or define a subject or object of a sentence. Sometimes the extra information given in the relative clause is necessary to define whom or what we are talking about, while other times it just gives us extra information.

Essential or necessary information:

> ***Last night I read the newest book.*** ["The newest book"? What book? This sentence is unclear. We need to define "the newest book" a bit better.] →

> ***Last night I read the newest book <u>that was written by Ian Rankin</u>.*** [The relative clause "that was written by Ian Rankin" helps to define "the newest book," since there can only be one "newest book" written by Ian Rankin.]

Nonessential or extra information:

> ***Last night I read a book.*** [We use the article "a" with nouns that have not yet been defined, so "a book" does not need information to define it. However, I can still give extra information about the book.] →

> ***Last night I read a book, <u>which was written by Ian Rankin</u>.*** [The relative clause "which was written by Ian Rankin" does not clearly define "a book," since Ian Rankin wrote many books. However, this relative clause does give extra information about the book.]

We often think of relative clauses as clauses that usually begin with the relative pronouns that, which, or who. However, in some relative clauses, we can reduce or shorten the clause by removing the relative pronoun and even changing the verb. Look at the following examples:

> 1. *correct: Last night I read the newest book that was written by Ian Rankin.*
> 2. *incorrect: Last night I read the newest book was written by Ian Rankin.*
> 3. *correct: Last night I read the newest book written by Ian Rankin.*

> 4. *correct: Last night I read a book, which was written by Ian Rankin.*
> 5. *incorrect: Last night I read a book, was written by Ian Rankin.*
> 6. *correct: Last night I read a book written by Ian Rankin.*

Reduced Relative Clauses can be formed from either essential or nonessential information. However, if the relative pronoun is the subject of the relative clause (Examples 1 & 4), you can reduce the clause by removing BOTH the relative pronoun AND the auxiliary verb (Examples 3 & 6). Be careful—you cannot remove ONLY the relative pronoun in these cases (Examples 2 & 5).

This rule is also true for making Reduced Relative Clauses with –ING verbs, such as verbs in the simple present or past tense, or in the present or past continuous tense. You can remove the relative pronoun and the auxiliary verb to reduce the clause.

> 7. *correct: The tomb was excavated by a man who was looking for King Tut.*
> 8. *incorrect: The tomb was excavated by a man was looking for King Tut.*
> 9. *correct: The tomb was excavated by a man looking for King Tut.*

B. **Look at these sentences from our reading. In each sentence, underline the Reduced Relative Clause. Then in the space at the end of the sentence, write the missing relative pronoun and the auxiliary and main verbs before they were reduced.**

1. While in the Holy Land, Stephens relied on a map drawn by a man named Frederick Catherwood. *(lines 22–23)* [**relative pronoun and auxiliary verb:** _____]

2. Catherwood showed Stephens a letter written by a Colonel Galindo that described his visit to the ancient ruins of the Mayan site of Palenque in Mexico. *(lines 25–27)* [**relative pronoun and auxiliary verb:** _____]

3. John Lloyd Stephens supposedly took possession of Copan, acquired for the fantastic sum of $50! *(lines 42–43)* [**relative pronoun and auxiliary verb:** _____]

4. In Stela B we see King 18 Rabbit holding one of the most important of the royal scepters. *(lines 70–71)* [**relative pronoun and auxiliary verb:** _____]

5. This need was fulfilled by farmers selecting different corn varieties. *(lines 105–106)* [**relative pronoun and auxiliary verb:** _____]

C. **Combine the following sentences, but write them as a single sentence with a Reduced Relative Clause.**

1. Our team in Ireland excavated many artifacts. These artifacts were classified according to their size, age, and function. _____
    _____

2. Somewhere in Olduvai Gorge the journalist found Louis Leakey. Leakey was searching for early human remains. _____
    _____

3. Mary Leakey discovered a prehistoric skull. This skull had been hidden under layers of rock and sand. _____
    _____

4. The ancient Jomon people of Japan stored food in pots. Those archaic pots were made from clay.
    _____
    _____

5. In the year 1711 an Italian peasant accidentally discovered the ancient city of Herculaneum. This city had been buried by a volcanic explosion in AD 79. _____
    _____

6. The volcano Vesuvius killed thousands of people. They were trying to escape the destruction of their city. _____
    _____

ARCHAEOLOGY

The things that people make and which archaeologists excavate are called artifacts. Artifacts are not just objects; they tell us something about the cultures that made them—about their beliefs, traditions, and rituals. Each of these images depicts an artifact from a different culture. Choose three of them and write a description. What are they? Who do you think made them? What was their purpose?

LITERATURE

The term "literature" comes from an ancient Greek word meaning "letters."
A "literate" person is someone who knows their "letters"; in other words,
someone who can read and write. Literature is a collection of artistic writings.
It could include stories, novels, poetry, even letters.

A.   What are the different genres or categories of literature? Write as many as you can think of.

     mystery

B.   Discuss the following questions in groups.

1.   Do you like to read? What kinds of things do you read? Do you read them for school? Work? Just for you, for the pleasure of reading?

2.   Do you have a favorite writer? A favorite book or story or poem? How about a favorite genre of literature? Have your tastes in literature changed over the years? How?

3.   Why is literature such an enduring part of culture? What is the benefit for a culture in producing and preserving texts and stories and novels and poetry?

4.   Do you write anything artistic? Have you ever composed a poem? Why did you write it? Have you ever written a story? What was it about?

C.   Using whatever resources are available to you—your classmates, a library, the Internet—write down the names of four authors who write literature in the English language and four authors who write in your language. Include the genre that they have written in and the title of one famous work they have composed.

	AUTHOR	GENRE	TITLE
1.			
2.			
3.			
4.			
5.			
6.			
7.			
8.			

LITERATURE   VOCABULARY 2.1

A. **The bold words below are our target vocabulary for Reading 1 in this unit. Among the many other words you see are synonyms. Not every word is a synonym for the vocabulary words, but each vocabulary word has one synonym. Match the vocabulary words to the correct synonyms. The first one has been done for you.**

B. **The EN- or EM- prefix generally means "to make" or "to give."**

enlarge → *en + large = to make bigger*

e.g., I asked the architect if he could *enlarge* the small back room so that I could use it as my study.

Use some of the following words with EN- or EM- to complete the sentences.

embody	enable	encourage	enliven	enslave	entomb
empower	encamp	enfold	enrich	enthrone	entrust

1. When the Spaniards arrived in Peru, they began to _____ the Inca, forcing them to serve the Spaniards and to dig for gold and silver.

2. There were so many people staying near the lake that we decided to _____ higher up in the mountain so that we could enjoy some peace and quiet.

3. I knew I would be in Turkey for three months and I was worried about my home in the US, so I _____ the keys of my home with my dependable best friend.

4. If you study English every day, this should _____ you not only to pass this class, but to be successful in your future college studies.

5. Millions of immigrants from all over the world have _____ American culture, benefitting this country in many ways.

C. **The root of the word "spectator" is SPEC, which means "look" or "see." The following words are all derived from the root word SPEC. Draw lines to match each word with an appropriate definition.**

1. circumspection
2. inspect
3. inspector
4. introspection
5. prospect
6. respect
7. specific
8. spectacular
9. spectator
10. speculate

a. *something to look forward to, such as an opportunity for success*

b. *looking at someone with consideration or regard*

c. *someone who watches something or looks on an event*

d. *being so impressive that everyone wants to see it*

e. *someone who looks into things carefully, like a detective*

f. *to look at something very closely or critically*

g. *looking inside oneself to understand things better*

h. *not general, but seen or known in a particular way*

i. *to try to guess or see what will happen in the future*

j. *looking around or taking everything into consideration*

D. **Now use nine of the words in Part C to fill in the blanks of the following short story.**

Joining the mafia was probably not the wisest decision Carlos had ever made, but what other

_____ **(1)** did he have? He had no real education, no skills that could land him a

good job with a decent salary. A guy like Carlos—nobody had _____ **(2)** for

him; everybody just looked down on him from day one! That is, until he joined the mob. Suddenly his

life was _____ **(3)**! He got everything he wanted, and everyone—everyone!—

treated him better. Even the big boss. Especially when Carlos managed to "disappear" the

_____ **(4)** who was getting too close to finding enough evidence to put the boss

away for life. Oh yeah, life for Carlos was pretty good now!

So why did he have to go and ruin it all by agreeing to a late night poker game … with the boss

himself?! It was his drinking that had done him in—too much alcohol, not enough brains. If only he had

shown more _____ **(5)**, Carlos wouldn't be in this mess now, sitting across the

table from the one man who could have Carlos iced with a single command. Carlos could not remember

the _____ **(6)** moment when he had done so, but at a particular time last night at

the bar, he had actually challenged the boss to a card game—the boss, who hated to lose!

Now here he was. Perhaps his last moment alive on this earth. Carlos, the drunk. He

_____ **(7)** his cards carefully, trying to imagine how he could get out of this. He

knew he couldn't just throw the game; the boss never went easy on men who crawled away from a fight.

All around the table, the _____ **(8)** could not keep their eyes off the game. They

knew that at any moment, something bad was going to happen. And all Carlos could do now was

_____ **(9)** on how it would happen—how he would die. Because win or lose, he

knew the boss would have him killed!

LITERATURE

Active reading can help you better understand a college text. Begin by discussing the questions below. Then carefully read "After Twenty Years" by O. Henry and the poem "Two Years Later" by W.B. Yeats. Take notes on the characters, ideas, and events you encounter and consider your response to the poem. Also select the best meaning for words highlighted in the right-hand column.

PREREADING DISCUSSION

1. The following short story and poem are about time and how things change as time passes. How have you changed over the last five years of your life? How about the last ten years? Twenty years?
2. Do you think someone's character or personality can change over time? Has yours changed? Have you ever known someone to change like that? Describe that person.
3. Have you ever met up with an old friend, someone you have not seen in a long time? Did you still feel close to that person? Was it a happy meeting? An awkward one? Perhaps a sad one?

The policeman on the beat moved up the avenue impressively. The impressiveness was habitual and not for show, for spectators were few. The time was barely 10 o'clock at night, but chilly gusts of wind with a taste of rain in them had well-nigh
5 de-peopled the streets.

Trying doors as he went, twirling his club with many intricate and artful movements, turning now and then to cast his watchful eye adown the pacific thoroughfare, the officer, with his stalwart form and slight swagger, made a fine picture of a
10 guardian of the peace. The vicinity was one that kept early hours. Now and then you might see the lights of a cigar store or of an all-night lunch counter; but the majority of the doors belonged to business places that had long since been closed.

When about midway of a certain block the policeman
15 suddenly slowed his walk. In the doorway of a darkened hardware store a man leaned, with an unlighted cigar in his mouth. As the policeman walked up to him the man spoke up quickly.

"It's all right, officer," he said, reassuringly. "I'm just waiting for a
20 friend. It's an appointment made twenty years ago. Sounds a little funny to you, doesn't it? Well, I'll explain if you'd like to make certain it's all straight. About that long ago there used to be a restaurant where this store stands—'Big Joe' Brady's restaurant."

"Until five years ago," said the policeman. "It was torn down then."

25 The man in the doorway struck a match and lit his cigar. The light showed a pale, square-jawed face with keen eyes, and a little white scar near his right eyebrow. His scarfpin was a large diamond, oddly set.

"Twenty years ago tonight," said the man, "I dined here at 'Big Joe' Brady's with Jimmy Wells, my best chum, and the finest chap in the world. He
30 and I were raised here in New York, just like two brothers, together. I was eighteen and Jimmy was twenty. The next morning I was to start for the West to make my fortune. You couldn't have dragged Jimmy out of New York; he thought it was the only place on earth. Well, we agreed that night that we would meet here again exactly twenty years from that date and time, no matter what our

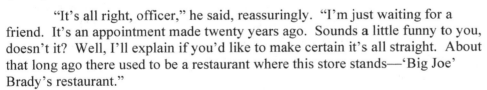

line 21: straight

a. honest
b. unbent
c. tidy

Another example:
I'm not sure what you are trying to say. Just be straight with me.

35 conditions might be or from what distance we might have to come. We figured
that in twenty years each of us ought to have our destiny worked out and our
fortunes made, whatever they were going to be."

"It sounds pretty interesting," said the policeman. "Rather a long time
between meets, though, it seems to me. Haven't you heard from your friend
40 since you left?"

"Well, yes, for a time we corresponded," said the other. "But after a
year or two we lost track of each other. You see, the West is a pretty big
proposition, and I kept hustling around over it pretty lively. But I know Jimmy
will meet me here if he's alive, for he always was the truest, staunchest old chap
45 in the world. He'll never forget. I came a thousand miles to stand in this door
tonight, and it's worth it if my old partner turns up."

The waiting man pulled out a handsome watch, the lids of it set with
small diamonds.

"Three minutes to ten," he announced. "It was exactly ten o'clock when
50 we parted here at the restaurant door."

"Did pretty well out West, didn't you?" asked the policeman.

"You bet! I hope Jimmy has done half as well. He was a kind of
plodder, though, good fellow as he was. I've had to compete with some of the
sharpest wits going to get my pile. A man gets in a groove in New York. It takes
55 the West to put a razor-edge on him."

The policeman twirled his club and took a step or two.

"I'll be on my way. Hope your friend comes around all right. Going to
call time on him sharp?"

"I should say not!" said the other. "I'll give him half an hour at least. If
60 Jimmy is alive on earth he'll be here by that time. So long, officer."

"Good night, sir," said the policeman, passing on along his beat, trying
doors as he went.

There was now a fine, cold drizzle falling, and the wind had risen from
its uncertain puffs into a steady blow. The few foot passengers astir in that
65 quarter hurried dismally and silently along with coat collars turned high and
pocketed hands. And in the door of the hardware store the man who had come a
thousand miles to fill an appointment, uncertain almost to absurdity, with the
friend of his youth, smoked his cigar and waited.

About twenty minutes he waited, and then a tall man in a long overcoat,
70 with collar turned up to his ears, hurried across from the opposite side of the
street. He went directly to the waiting man.

"Is that you, Bob?" he asked, doubtfully.

"Is that you, Jimmy Wells?" cried the man in the door.

"Bless my heart!" exclaimed the new arrival, grasping both the other's
75 hands with his own. "It's Bob, sure as fate. I was certain I'd find you here if you
were still in existence. Well, well, well!—twenty years is a long time. The old
restaurant's gone, Bob; I wish it had lasted, so we could have had another dinner
there. How has the West treated you, old man?"

---

line 35: figure

a. number
b. shape
c. calculate

Another example:
Takayuki figured it would take him 3 hours to write his paper.

---

line 43: keep

a. to hold
b. to continue
c. to stay

Another example:
Why do you keep complaining about your job? Get a new one!

---

line 61: beat

a. precinct
b. strike
c. tired

Another example:
I'm not doing anything about this. This isn't even my beat.

80 "Bully; it has given me everything I asked it for. You've changed lots, Jimmy. I never thought you were so tall by two or three inches."

"Oh, I grew a bit after I was twenty."

"Doing well in New York, Jimmy?"

85 "Moderately. I have a position in one of the city departments. Come on, Bob; we'll go around to a place I know of, and have a good long talk about old times."

The two men started up the street, arm in arm. The man from the West, his egotism enlarged by success, was beginning to outline the history of his career. The other, submerged in his overcoat, listened with interest.

90 At the corner stood a drug store, brilliant with electric lights. When they came into this glare, each of them turned simultaneously to gaze upon the other's face.

The man from the West stopped suddenly and released his arm.

"You're not Jimmy Wells," he snapped. "Twenty years is a long time, but not long enough to change a man's nose from a Roman to a pug."

95 "It sometimes changes a good man into a bad one," said the tall man. "You've been under arrest for ten minutes, 'Silky' Bob. Chicago thinks you may have dropped over our way and wires us she wants to have a chat with you. Going quietly, are you? That's sensible. Now, before we go on to the station here's a note I was asked to hand you. You may read it here at the window. It's
100 from Patrolman Wells."

The man from the West unfolded the little piece of paper handed him. His hand was steady when he began to read, but it trembled a little by the time he had finished. The note was rather short.

105 *Bob: I was at the appointed place on time. When you struck the match to light your cigar I saw it was the face of the man wanted in Chicago. Somehow I couldn't do it myself, so I went around and got a plain clothes man to do the job.*

JIMMY

TWO YEARS LATER, by W.B. Yeats

Has no one said those daring
Kind eyes should be more learn'd?
Or warned you how despairing
The moths are when they are burned?
I could have warned you; but you are young,
So we speak a different tongue.

O you will take whatever's offered
And dream that all the world's a friend.
Suffer as your mother suffered,
Be as broken in the end.
But I am old and you are young,
And I speak a barbarous tongue.

---

line 89: brilliant

a. *very bright*
b. *very clear*
c. *very intelligent*

Another example:
Well-lit to celebrate the New Year, the hall was absolutely brilliant.

---

tongue

a. *speak*
b. *language*
c. *organ of the mouth*

Another example:
She spoke such perfect Chinese, but this was not her native tongue.

LITERATURE

A. *How would you interpret the following sentences from the story? Circle the letter of the sentence closest in meaning to the sentence from the story.*

1. The policeman on the beat moved up the avenue impressively. *(lines 1–2)*
   a. The policeman was terribly beaten on the street.
   b. The policeman was very impressed with his job on the street.
   c. The policeman on the job was walking impressively on the street.

2. …chilly gusts of wind with a taste of rain in them had well-nigh de-peopled the streets. *(lines 4–5)*
   a. People in the windy street were tasting the rain.
   b. The wind was blowing rain into people's faces.
   c. The wet wind had made most people leave the street.

3. …the officer … made a fine picture of a guardian of the peace. *(lines 8–10)*
   a. The policeman was a good example of an officer of the law.
   b. The policeman was a handsome and peaceful man.
   c. The policeman made a very good drawing of a guardian.

4. The vicinity was one that kept early hours. *(line 10)*
   a. People in the neighborhood tended to be on time.
   b. The vicinity was always opened early.
   c. Businesses in the area usually closed early.

5. Well, I'll explain if you'd like to make certain it's all straight. *(line 21)*
   a. You might want to make sure I am telling the story correctly.
   b. I will tell you if you want to make sure I'm not causing any trouble.
   c. I can tell you how to make this straight if you'd like.

6. He and I were raised here … just like two brothers, together. *(lines 29–30)*
   a. He and I were raised here together as if we were brothers.
   b. He and I were picked up together here.
   c. He and I grew up together here, just like two brothers I know.

7. But after a year or two we lost track of each other. *(lines 41–42)*
   a. After a couple years, I stopped following him.
   b. After one or two years we couldn't find each other anymore.
   c. After a year or two we stopped communicating.

8. … the West is a pretty big proposition, and I kept hustling around over it pretty lively. *(lines 42–43)*
   a. There's a lot to do in the West and I was very busy.
   b. The West is large and attractive, and I moved around a lot.
   c. I had a proposal to cheat a lot of people in the West.

9. I hope Jimmy has done half as well. *(line 52)*
   a. I hope Jimmy is only half as happy as I am.
   b. I hope Jimmy has achieved half of his goals by now.
   c. I hope Jimmy has been at least half as successful as me.

10. I have a position in one of the city departments. *(line 83)*
    a. I work at a department store in the city.
    b. I have my own place in a neighborhood of the city.
    c. I am employed by the city government.

11. I went around and got a plain clothes man to do the job. *(lines 106–07)*
    a. I hired a man in plain clothing to work for me.
    b. I told a policeman in civilian clothes to do the job.
    c. I looked around and found a simple clothing salesman.

B. Which of the following statements best summarizes the surprise ending of the story?

1. Despite their committed friendship, Jimmy failed to keep his appointment with Bob in New York because he could not bear to see how his friend had changed for the bad.

2. Although so many things had changed in Bob's life, he still took the long trip back to New York just to see his dear friend from 20 years ago.

3. Jimmy did keep the appointment with Bob, but when he recognized Bob as a wanted criminal, he pretended to be someone else so that another officer could arrest Bob.

C. Write your answers to the following questions about the story "After Twenty Years"?

1. Where did Bob and Jimmy grow up? _____

2. What was Bob and Jimmy's relationship? _____

3. Why did Bob travel to the West? _____

4. What kind of work did the man pretending to be Jimmy say he was doing in New York? _____
    _____

5. What kind of work was Jimmy really doing? _____

6. What kind of work was Bob doing? _____

7. Which of the two men was older? _____

8. What was important about "'Big Joe' Brady's"? _____
    _____

9. What agreement did Bob and Jimmy make? _____
    _____

10. Why did they choose "twenty years" for their meeting? _____
    _____

11. According to Bob, how do people change in the West? _____
    _____

12. How does Bob finally realize that the second man is not Jimmy? _____
    _____

13. What is the second man's job? _____

14. In his note, Jimmy wrote, "Somehow I couldn't do it myself, so I went around and got a plain clothes man to do the job." What do you think this means? Why didn't Jimmy arrest "Silky" Bob himself? _____
    _____
    _____
    _____

LITERATURE

A. REAL AND UNREAL CONDITIONALS

Conditional sentences can describe what will or might happen in the future as well as what might have happened in the past. Look at the following sentences. How are they structurally different from one another?

   a.   If I go to bed late tonight, I will be tired tomorrow.
   b.   If I went to bed late tonight, I would be tired tomorrow.

Is there any difference in meaning between the two sentences above? Can you explain the difference?

Do the following conditional sentences describe real or unreal (imagined) situations? Circle REAL or UNREAL for each sentence.

1.   REAL   UNREAL   If Sherry passes this test, she will get an A grade in this class.

2.   REAL   UNREAL   If you need a ride to the airport, I will drive you.

3.   REAL   UNREAL   If we had more money, we would go on vacation this summer.

4.   REAL   UNREAL   If Keith visits me next month, I will take him to the temple.

5.   REAL   UNREAL   If Maria knew how hard Statistics is, she would not major in Math.

6.   REAL   UNREAL   If this computer breaks down again, I will buy a new one.

B. TIME AND CONDITIONALS

Conditionals are not just used to explain real or imagined situations at one time; they can be used to describe the present, past, and future. Look at the following examples. Notice the verb tenses and the times indicated by such phrases as "tomorrow" and "last week."

   a.   If I go to bed late, I am tired the next day. **[real in the present and in general]**
   b.   If I go to bed late tonight, I will be tired tomorrow. **[real in the future]**
   c.   If I went to bed late tonight, I would be tired tomorrow. **[imagined in the future]**
   d.   If I had gone to bed late last week, I would have been tired all week. **[imagined in the past]**

Complete the following sentences with the appropriate verb tense based on the time indicated.

1.   I will give you a call tonight if I _____ *(have)* time.

2.   If I _____ *(study)* too much, I always get a headache.

3.   I would enjoy this movie more if the story _____ *(not be)* so ridiculous. I can't believe it got an award!

4.   If Jeremy isn't working tomorrow, I'm sure he _____ *(come)* to Melissa's birthday party.

5.   If your presentation _____ *(not impress)* the teacher so much, I doubt you would have gotten such a high grade.

6.   If Teresa had not missed her flight, she _____ *(arrive)* on time yesterday.

30

C. **Look at these sentences. Mark the correct boxes to indicate 1) if they are real or unreal conditionals, and 2) what time they refer to.**

1. Well, I'll explain if you'd like to make certain it's all straight.
   - ☐ real
   - ☐ unreal
   - ☐ past
   - ☐ present
   - ☐ future

2. But I know Jimmy will meet me here if he's alive.
   - ☐ real
   - ☐ unreal
   - ☐ past
   - ☐ present
   - ☐ future

3. I came a thousand miles to stand in this door tonight, and it's worth it if my old partner turns up.
   - ☐ real
   - ☐ unreal
   - ☐ past
   - ☐ present
   - ☐ future

4. If you went to Turkey for your vacation, you would see the most stunning historical monuments!
   - ☐ real
   - ☐ unreal
   - ☐ past
   - ☐ present
   - ☐ future

5. There would have been enough food for everyone if we had gone shopping before the party.
   - ☐ real
   - ☐ unreal
   - ☐ past
   - ☐ present
   - ☐ future

D. **Use your imagination to complete the following sentences based on your understanding of the story.**

1. If Bob had not lit his cigar in the dark, Jimmy _____

   _____

2. If Bob had stayed in New York instead of traveling West, _____

   _____

3. If Bob had realized that the man with him was not Jimmy, _____

   _____

4. If Bob had not waited 20 minutes more after Jimmy left, _____

   _____

5. If Bob and Jimmy had not agreed to meet again after 20 years, _____

   _____

E. **Now complete these sentences about your own life.**

1. If I had not come to the United States, _____

   _____

2. If I were very wealthy, _____

   _____

3. If I could live anywhere in the world, _____

   _____

LITERATURE

Choose from the following options for your journal writing assignment:

1. We all change with time, wouldn't you say? We experience more than just physical changes; we change inside—our characters. At least, some people believe so. Do you think it's true? Start this writing assignment by making a list of at least ten things that can change in a person's life.

    1) _____   6) _____
    2) _____   7) _____
    3) _____   8) _____
    4) _____   9) _____
    5) _____   10) _____

    Now choose at least three of these things and write about how they have changed in YOUR life.

2. Cities can change as well, as do countries. In the story, Bob left New York and returned 20 years later to find a beloved restaurant closed down. Perhaps you have seen changes in your own home town or your native country. Describe how a place you know well has changed over time. What kinds of changes have occurred? Have these changes improved the place you are describing or made it worse? How have these changes affected your feelings about the place? Did you enjoy living there before? Would you still want to live there now?

3. Bob and Jimmy agreed to meet after 20 years because they believed that would be enough time for at least one of them to make his fortune—to get rich. Really? Twenty years? Do you think you'll be rich in 20 years? Assuming you might want to be rich someday, describe what you think is the best way to accomplish this goal. What is your plan for making your fortune? Is it more like Jimmy's life or Bob's? And once you've got your fortune, what do you plan to do with it? If you could hit it big, how would you spend your money?

4. Look at the following words from the story "After Twenty Years." Choose five of these words and write about a person, condition, or situation that matches or illustrates the word.

    1) absurd   8) guardian
    2) chilly   9) impressive
    3) despair   10) intricate
    4) destiny   11) keen
    5) dismal   12) sensible
    6) egotism   13) suffer
    7) fortune   14) swagger

LITERATURE   VOCABULARY 2.2

A. *Here are our target vocabulary for Reading 2 in this unit:*

ashamed	culminate	expose	vision
barren	declare	senile	weep
comfort	demon	torment	wicked

B. *Each of the sentences below illustrates one of our vocabulary words for this chapter. Write the correct vocabulary word next to the sentence that illustrates the meaning of that word. Then underline the synonym for the vocabulary word in the sentence.*

1. _____ It was not out of love that Ronald married Clarice, but for some evil intention that he was concealing.

2. _____ The celebration for 4 July last year concluded with a fantastic fireworks display.

3. _____ People used to believe that abnormal behavior was actually caused by some sort of devil rather than by a psychological illness.

4. _____ When settlers from Virginia arrived in Nebraska, they were shocked by how lifeless the land seemed to be, with no trees or bushes around.

5. _____ The police investigation has uncovered a terrible amount of corruption in the local government.

6. _____ When I arrived at the funeral, I found Aunt Sara sobbing in the corner by herself so I went to comfort her.

7. _____ The doctor declared that Uncle Rudy was just too old and mentally infirm to drive a car anymore and so he lost his driver's license.

8. _____ The brutality of the conquering army was obvious in how they tortured the poor people of our city.

9. _____ The priest described an apparition he claimed to have seen of an angel standing before him.

10. _____ Terry was really hit hard by the loss of his job, so I decided to drive by his house and console him.

11. _____ The king proclaimed that the first son of every family was required to join the army in preparation for war.

12. _____ I was so embarrassed about failing the test that I didn't tell anyone, not even my best friend.

C. *Write the letter of the word in each list that best completes the sentence.*

1. Mom bought a nice new _____ so that she can wrap up and stay warm on a winter's night.

2. When are they going to fix the air conditioner in this place. It's so _____ in this awful heat!

3. Thank you for your kind letter after my cousin passed away. What you wrote to me was very _____.

    a. *comfort*
    b. *comfortable*
    c. *comforter*
    d. *comforting*
    e. *uncomfortable*

4. The _____ issued by the government states that all men are created equal.

5. Your taxes were so high this year because you _____ that you only had one person to take care of. You actually have three.

6. The mayor has _____ that every Friday his staff must bicycle to work—no cars on Fridays.

    f. *declare*
    g. *declarative*
    h. *declaration*
    i. *misdeclare*
    j. *redeclare*

D. *Now use ten of our vocabulary words from this chapter to fill in the blanks of the following short story.*

Morgan McConnell was by no means a happy man, especially since his wife had died. He was not a _____ **(1)** man, certainly not evil, but he was not at all well. That much was clear. And as the years passed, the townspeople of Kilmadock became convinced that Morgan had become _____ **(2)**. His infirmity was so terrible, that he would sit for hours in the middle of his garden, just sit there and _____ **(3)** like a man who has just lost everything and everyone he had ever loved. The tears rolled down his face until suddenly he seemed to become so _____ **(4)** of his own behavior that he would jump up, run into his house, and slam the door shut behind him as if he could no longer bear to _____ **(5)** himself and his sadness to the public view.

One winter night when Morgan had not been seen for some time, I took it upon myself to visit him at his cottage. The garden was quite _____ **(6)**, with no sign of life whatsoever, not even the vines that survive the cold. But what disturbed me even more was to enter the door and find the old man lying upon his bed twisting and turning like a man possessed. And indeed I had to wonder if perhaps some terrifying _____ **(7)** had entered his heart, some devil controlling his every move. His eyes were wide open and full of fear as if he could see a frightening _____ **(8)** floating above him where he lay on his bed. Slowly I approached him, staring at this poor man, and I wondered, 'What is it that _____ **(9)** him so?' Then suddenly he grabbed my arm and pointed at the ceiling and _____ **(10)**, "There she is! She has come for me!" And all at once, he screamed and died.

LITERATURE

Discuss the questions below with your peers. Then carefully read "Senility" by Sherwood Anderson and the succeeding poems by Edgar Allen Poe and H.P. Lovecraft, and the free verse poems. Take notes on the characters, ideas, and events you encounter and consider your response to the poems. Also select the best meaning for words highlighted in the right-hand column.

PREREADING DISCUSSION

1. What is "senility"? Do you know anyone who has experienced senility?
2. What are the consequences of aging? What happens to us as we get older?
3. How are the elderly treated in your culture? How do you think they are treated here?
4. Are you worried about getting older? Why or why not?
5. What kind of life do you expect to have when you are older?

(1)   He was an old man and he sat on the steps of the railroad station in a small Kentucky town.

A well-dressed man, some traveler from the city, approached and stood before him.

5   The old man became self-conscious.

His smile was like the smile of a very young child. His face was all sunken and wrinkled and he had a huge nose.

(2)   "Have you any coughs, colds, consumption or bleeding sickness?" he asked. In his voice there was a pleading quality.

10   The stranger shook his head. The old man arose.

"The sickness that bleeds is a terrible nuisance," he said. His tongue protruded from between his teeth and he rattled it about. He put his hand on the stranger's arm and laughed.

(3)   "Bully, pretty," he exclaimed. "I cure them all—coughs, colds,
15   consumption and the sickness that bleeds. I take warts from the hand—I cannot explain how I do it—it is a mystery—I charge nothing—my name is Tom—do you like me?"

The stranger was cordial. He nodded his head. The old man became reminiscent. "My father was a hard man," he declared. "He was like me, a
20   blacksmith by trade, but he wore a plug hat. When the corn was high he said to the poor, 'go into the fields and pick' but when the war came he made a rich man pay five dollars for a bushel of corn.

(4)   "I married against his will. He came to me and he said, 'Tom, I do not like that girl.'"

25   "'But I love her,' I said.

"'I don't,' he said.

"My father and I sat on a log. He was a pretty man and wore a plug hat. 'I will get the license,' I said.

"'I will give you no money,' he said.

A blacksmith at work

35

30 (5)   "My marriage cost me twenty-one dollars—I worked in the corn—it rained and the horses were blind—the clerk said, 'Are you over twenty-one?' I said, 'Yes,' and she said, 'Yes.' We had chalked it on our shoes. My father said, 'I give you your freedom.' We had no money. My marriage cost twenty-one dollars. She is dead."

35   The old man looked at the sky. It was evening and the sun had set. The sky was all mottled with grey clouds. "I paint beautiful pictures and give them away," he declared. "My brother is in the penitentiary. He killed a man who called him an ugly name."

Eastern State Penitentiary in Philadelphia

40 (6)   The decrepit old man held his hands before the face of the stranger. He opened and shut them. They were black with grime. "I pick out warts," he explained plaintively. "They are as soft as your hands."

        "I play on an accordion. You are thirty-seven years
45 old. I sat beside my brother in the penitentiary. He is a pretty man with pompadour hair. 'Albert,' I said, 'are you sorry you killed a man?' 'No,' he said, 'I am not sorry. I would kill ten, a hundred, a thousand!'"

    (7)   The old man began to weep and to wipe his hands with a soiled
50 handkerchief. He attempted to take a chew of tobacco and his false teeth became displaced. He covered his mouth with his hands and was ashamed.

        "I am old. You are thirty-seven years old but I am older than that," he whispered.

        "My brother is a bad man—he is full of hate—he is pretty and has
55 pompadour hair, but he would kill and kill. I hate old age—I am ashamed that I am old.

    (8)   "I have a pretty new wife. I wrote her four letters and she replied. She came here and we married—I love to see her walk—O, I buy her pretty clothes.

        "Her foot is not straight—it is twisted—my first wife is dead—I pick
60 warts off the hand with my fingers and no blood comes—I cure coughs, colds, consumption and the sickness that bleeds—people can write to me and I answer the letters—if they send me no money it is no matter—all is free."

        Again the old man wept and the stranger tried to comfort him. "You are a happy man?" the stranger asked.

65 (9)   "Yes," said the old man, "and a good man too. Ask everywhere about me—my name is Tom, a blacksmith—my wife walks prettily although she has a twisted foot—I have bought her a long dress—she is thirty and I am seventy-five—she has many pairs of shoes—I have bought them for her, but her foot is twisted—I buy straight shoes—

70   "She thinks I do not know—everybody thinks Tom does not know—I have bought her a long dress that comes down to the ground—my name is Tom, a blacksmith—I am seventy-five and I hate old age—I take warts off the hands and no blood comes—people may write to me and I answer the letters—all is free."

---

line 49: soil

a. earth
b. dirty
c. dust

Another example:
These soiled shirts need to be washed again.

---

line 59: twisted

a. crooked
b. winding
c. perverse

Another example:
I cannot use my ruler anymore. It got twisted when I sat on it.

LITERATURE

A Dream within a Dream, Edgar Allan Poe

Take this kiss upon the brow!
And, in parting from you now,
Thus much let me avow—
You are not wrong, who deem
5   That my days have been a dream;
Yet if hope has flown away
In a night, or in a day,
In a vision, or in none,
Is it therefore the less gone?
10 All that we see or seem
Is but a dream within a dream.

I stand amid the roar
Of a surf-tormented shore,
15 And I hold within my hand
Grains of the golden sand—
How few! yet how they creep
Through my fingers to the deep,
While I weep—while I weep!
20 O God! can I not grasp
Them with a tighter clasp?
O God! can I not save
One from the pitiless wave?
Is all that we see or seem
25 But a dream within a dream?

Despair, H. P. Lovecraft

O'er the midnight moorlands crying,
Through the cypress forests sighing,
In the night-wind madly flying,
Hellish forms with streaming hair;
5   In the barren branches creaking,
By the stagnant swamp-pools speaking,
Past the shore-cliffs ever shrieking,
Damned demons of despair.
Once, I think I half remember,
10 Ere the grey skies of November
Quenched my youth's aspiring ember,
Lived there such a thing as bliss;
Skies that now are dark were beaming,
Bold and azure, splendid seeming
15 Till I learn'd it all was dreaming—
Deadly drowsiness of Dis.
But the stream of Time, swift flowing,
Brings the torment of half-knowing—
Dimly rushing, blindly going
20 Past the never-trodden lea;

And the voyager, repining,
Sees the wicked death-fires shining,
Hears the wicked petrel's whining
25 As he helpless drifts to sea.
Evil wings in ether beating;
Vultures at the spirit eating;
Things unseen forever fleeting
Black against the leering sky.
30 Ghastly shades of bygone gladness,
Clawing fiends of future sadness,
Mingle in a cloud of madness
Ever on the soul to lie.
Thus the living, lone and sobbing,
35 In the throes of anguish throbbing,
With the loathsome Furies robbing
Night and noon of peace and rest.
But beyond the groans and grating
Of abhorrent Life, is waiting
40 Sweet Oblivion, culminating
All the years of fruitless quest.

There are different forms that poetry can take. We often think of poetry as rhyming, as with the verses above from Edgar Allen Poe and H.P. Lovecraft. However, not all poetry rhymes. Poetry that is not bound to a particular rhyming or metric pattern is known as free verse. Consider the following verses.

painted stars

i have seen these stars before
painted on brittle walls
that wept when summer came
wept for the passing spring
knowing that this time of ours
would never come again

my own life

once world weary, these feet
now lifting flowing forward
in gratefully certain rhythm
caressing the eager earth
with most ambitious steps
dreading nothing, ever hopeful
longing, loving, defining
my own life

progress

wood knows more of this
than you or surely me
trees stretching on and on
in rooted certainty

and yet you deny their voice
hearing only and often
the steadily clinking clacking sound
of coin on coin on coin

when you have done denuding
the lonely soil around us
and assessed the worthy footage
bend one knee at very least

and touch the hardening earth

mother

although i had indeed been warned
to prepare for the worst that day
i know now with painful certainty
that the worst was not that moment
seeing her cancered body dying there
in that cold unfeeling hospital bed
but rather thinking of all the days
the years that had quietly passed
while we had been apart

time

in utter confusion
time stumbled forth
like an agèd crone
quivering and lone
her mind mocking me
her skin cracked and
immensely disagreeable

laughter

in your gentle eyes
i have witnessed
the birth of hope

the departure of pain
fear extinguished
in smiles once shy

opening now like lilies
floating in a pool
of brightest laughter

LITERATURE

A. Complete the following statements based on information from the text.

1. A traveler who came from _____ spoke to the old man.

2. The old man smiled like _____

3. The old man declared that he can cure _____

4. The old man's name was _____.

5. Tom charged _____ to help people.

6. Tom had the same profession as _____.

7. Tom's father did not want Tom to marry his first wife, so he _____

    _____

8. It cost Tom _____ to get married.

9. Tom's brother was in _____ because he _____

10. Tom became ashamed because _____

11. Tom's new wife was _____ years old.

12. Tom bought her many straight shoes even though _____

B. So much of literature requires the reader to do more than just look for facts, the way you might with a biology or a computer science textbook. Literature requires a different kind of reading. Especially with poetry, the reader needs to use creative thinking and careful interpretation to try to understand what the poet is trying to say. How would you interpret the following passages from the poetry we have read? In your notebook, write what you think the following texts mean.

(1)
Is all that we see or seem
But a dream within a dream? *(Poe)*

(2)
In the barren branches creaking,
By the stagnant swamp-pools speaking,
Past the shore-cliffs ever shrieking,
Damned demons of despair. *(Lovecraft)*

(3)
Ghastly shades of bygone gladness,
Clawing fiends of future sadness,
Mingle in a cloud of madness
Ever on the soul to lie. *(Lovecraft)*

(4)
wood knows more of this
than you or surely me
trees stretching on and on
in rooted certainty *(free verse)*

(5)
in utter confusion
time stumbled forth
like an agèd crone
quivering and lone *(free verse)*

(6)
i have seen these stars before
painted on brittle walls
that wept when summer came *(free verse)*

C. *When you learn the vocabulary of a new language, you must learn all the parts of speech: nouns, verbs, adjectives, adverbs, prepositions, pronouns, conjunctions, and interjections. However, as you use these words and phrases, you begin to notice that certain parts of speech play a lesser or greater role in communication depending on the context and purpose of language use. In literature you find a greater number and variety of ADJECTIVES and ADVERBS being used by writers, who are more keen on fully describing people, places, and things in such a way that the reader can better imagine them. For example, in the first line of the story "Senility" there are two simple adjectives:*

He was an <u>old</u> man and he sat on the steps of the railroad station in a <u>small</u> Kentucky town.

In each of the following sentences adapted from the story, underline the ADJECTIVES and ADVERBS. Then circle the nouns that the ADJECTIVES describe, and the verbs or adjectives that the ADVERBS describe.

1. His face was all sunken and wrinkled and he had a huge nose.

2. "The sickness that bleeds is a terrible nuisance," he said.

3. The stranger was cordial. He nodded his head gently. The old man became reminiscent.

4. It was evening and the sun had slowly set. The sky was all mottled with grey clouds.

5. "I pick out warts," he explained plaintively.

6. He attempted to take a chew of tobacco and his false teeth became displaced.

7. I hate old age—I am so ashamed that I am old.

8. I have a pretty new wife. I wrote her four letters and she replied.

9. Her foot is not straight—it is quite twisted—my first wife is dead.

10. My wife walks prettily although she has a twisted foot—I recently bought her a long dress.

D. *When you learn new adjectives, pay attention to the nouns that are described by these adjectives so that you can use them correctly when you speak or write. Look at the following rows of words. Each row begins with an adjective, which is followed by four nouns. It is appropriate to use the adjective with three of those nouns. Circle the one noun that we usually do NOT describe with that adjective. Work with a partner and use a printed or online dictionary to help you with this.*

1. twisted	idea	limb	imagination	planet
2. cordial	invitation	milk	man	discussion
3. barren	desert	landscape	holiday	woman
4. wicked	people	hope	behavior	witch
5. unfamiliar	acquaintance	territory	subject	surroundings
6. helpless	invalid	argument	situation	victim
7. desperate	indifference	killer	fear	need
8. persistent	noise	cough	young man	surrender
9. intricate	machine	puzzle	pattern	mountain
10. absurd	explanation	success	claim	idea

LITERATURE

A. PUNCTUATION IN LITERATURE

When you first began studying English, no doubt you became aware of the comma and period as the most common punctuation marks in written English. Although they are so common, even native speakers of English have difficulty determining when to use them correctly, especially the comma. If you still make mistakes with commas, don't feel bad—many people make such mistakes.

However, when you read literature, you begin to encounter other types of punctuation that you may not be so familiar with. Look at the following passage and circle one example of every type of punctuation that you find. Can you name each one? How many different types are there?

> *It was Friday—end of the week at last! When I got home from school, I was so hungry and tired. Every Friday I have a class at the college that lasts three hours. What was I thinking? I mean, who can handle a three-hour class every Friday, right?*
>
> *When I walked in the door—and of course the TV was on—I just wanted to sit down and eat something. So I crashed on the couch next to the laziest roommate I have ever had—Carl—and asked him, "Have we got anything to eat?"*
>
> *Carl looked at me like I was crazy or something. He shook his blond-haired head and said, "Steven said to tell you, 'It's your turn to go shopping.'"*
>
> *'My turn?' I thought. 'You've got to be kidding!'*
>
> *"Fine!" I exclaimed, heading for the door. "I'm going. But don't expect me—are you listening?—to bring you anything!"*

B. Write the names of the following punctuation marks.

Name	*Symbol*	*Example*
1. _____	.	*I was so hungry and tired.*
2. _____	,	*I mean, who can handle*
3. _____	?	*What was I thinking?*
4. _____	!	*end of the week at last!*
5. _____	-	*a three-hour class*
6. _____	—	*I walked in the door—and of course*
7. _____	'	*It's your turn*
8. _____	' '	*'My turn?' I thought.*
9. _____	" "	*"Fine!" I exclaimed*

41

C. HYPHENS AND DASHES

Look at the following clauses. Notice where the hyphens are used. Write the letter of the correct reason for using a hyphen in that sentence.

1. _____ Who can handle a three-hour class every Friday?

2. _____ He shook his blond-haired head

3. _____ My marriage cost twenty-one dollars. *(lines 33–34)*

4. _____ I stand amid the roar / Of a surf-tormented shore *(lines 15–16)*

5. _____ In the barren branches creaking, / By the stagnant swamp-pools speaking *(lines 36–37)*

6. _____ I am seventy-five and I hate old age. *(line 72)*

7. _____ a boulevard recollecting shine / a charcoal's tall-tale

a.   combining two or more words together to create an adjective before a noun

b.   creating a complex number

c.   emphasizing the connection between two words

Unlike hyphens, dashes are never used to connect two words. Rather, we tend to use dashes for one of three reasons, stated in the following table. Once again, write the letter of the reason that matches the example sentences you see here.

8. _____ It was Friday—end of the week at last!

9. _____ When I walked in the door—and of course the TV was on—I just wanted to sit down and eat something.

10. _____ So I crashed on the couch next to the laziest roommate I have ever had—Carl—and asked him, "Have we got anything to eat?"

11. _____ "I'm going. But don't expect me—are you listening?—to bring you anything!"

12. _____ "I cure them all—coughs, colds, consumption and the sickness that bleeds." *(lines 14–15)*

13. _____ "My marriage cost me twenty-one dollars—I worked in the corn—it rained and the horses were blind." *(lines 30–31)*

14. _____ in parting from you now, thus much let me avow— you are not wrong *(lines 4–6)*

15. _____ "My brother is a bad man—he is full of hate—he is pretty and has pompadour hair." *(lines 54–55)*

d.   indicating an interruption, especially when quoting spoken English

e.   connecting a name or word with a definition or description of it (you can use commas for this as well, but the dashes give greater emphasis)

f.   giving extra information within a sentence (just as we do with parentheses)

D. QUOTATION MARKS

You will very often encounter quotation marks in reading literature, since quotation marks are the necessary punctuation that tells a reader when the author is writing or copying what someone has said or written elsewhere. If you write a story in which two people are speaking to one another, then you will probably use quotation marks. As a college student, you will also need to use quotation marks whenever you write a college essay in which you copy information from another source. Quotation marks will show your teacher that those sentences are not your sentences; that they are actually copied, for example from a book that you have read for your class.

In both of the stories we have read in this chapter, you have seen extensive use of double quotation marks and even some single quotation marks to show a dialogue—two people speaking. Use single quotation marks when you are writing a quote in which the speaker is quoting someone else. Look at these sentences:

1. *He shook his head and said, "Steven left you a message."*

2. *He shook his head and said, "Steven said to tell you, 'It's your turn to go shopping.'"*

Single quotation marks are also used to show NOT what someone is saying, but instead what they are thinking.

1. *"My turn?" I said. "You've got to be kidding!"*

2. *'My turn?' I thought. 'You've got to be kidding!'*

E. PUNCTUATION PRACTICE

The following passage is missing some essential punctuation, including commas, apostrophes, hyphens, dashes, single and double quotation marks, and question marks. Write in all the missing punctuation marks. Look again at the examples above; notice how the quotation mark comes after the period or other punctuation at the end of a quote.

Mark looked at his watch again. It was 10 00 o clock which meant it was time to make the call his weekly telephone call to his parents back in San Francisco. And he had never felt so nervous before.

You ve got to stop feeling this way he thought to himself. You re thirty two years old. You re a grown man. You can make your own decisions.

It was true of course. He was an adult there was no doubt about that and there was no reason for him to back down now. This was his life and his parents would just have to accept his decision. They would not like it but in the end it was indeed his decision to make. So he picked up the old fashioned phone and dialed the number.

Hello his father answered after only one ring. Mark imagined his father sitting there beside the phone just waiting for the call.

Hi Dad. How are you

Marky it s so good to hear your voice son his father declared. You know your mother was just saying It s about time Marky called.

Yeah Dad Mark said. Hey is Mom there I need to tell you two something.

LITERATURE

Choose from the following options for your journal writing assignment:

1. **POEMS**: Poetry may seem like a difficult thing to write, but we are all capable of composing poems. Even if you have never done it before, I'd like you to give it a try now. Let's start with something simple—colors and feelings.

red	green	blue
yellow	white	
black	pink	orange
brown	happy	
sad	afraid	angry
nervous	excited	
suspicious	desperate	hopeful

Choose any color or feeling you want and write a poem about it. However, you cannot use the name of the color or feeling in your poem. Instead, describe it—its feeling, its texture, its qualities, its effect on you. For example, what color do you think I am describing here:

> *The dome of the sky*
> *spreads warmly above*
> *hovering over me*
> *watching my days*

After you have composed your first poem, do the same thing with two more colors or feelings. When you are finished, share your poems with your peer group and see if they can guess what colors or feelings you have described.

2. **STORY**: For this writing assignment, I want you to compose a short story. You can choose whatever theme you want for your story, but if it helps you to decide, maybe you should write about the kind of themes we have been reading about in this chapter. Here are some common themes in literature. Look through them, think about them. If any of them seem interesting to you, circle them.

identity	change	humor
friendship	shame	
death	fear	love
family	pride	
childhood	old age	betrayal
journey	courage	
loss	desire	culture

Find a theme that works for you. If you do not like any of these, then choose your own. Think about the story you want to tell. Create at least two characters for your story, and write about something that happens to them. In your story, you must include dialogue.

MYTHOLOGY

Joseph Campbell, a US American expert on mythology and comparative religion, once described mythology as the literature of the spirit. What do you think he meant by that? What is mythology?

Look at the following images and discuss them with your peers. Who or what do you think they represent? Gods? Spirits? Demons? What cultures created them? What special powers might they have? What kind of stories would be told about them? What lessons could people learn from them?

MYTHOLOGY   VOCABULARY 3.1

A. **Here are our target vocabulary for Reading 1 in this unit:**

animated	assume	fundamental	obvious
approach	despite	individual	possess
aspect	eventually	injury	responsibility

B. **Using a dictionary to help you, circle the word in each row that is a synonym for the vocabulary words.**

1. **animated**	alive	watch	created
2. **approach**	travel from	come near	believe in
3. **aspect**	feature	need	surface
4. **assume**	know	suppose	theory
5. **despite**	because of	assuming that	in spite of
6. **eventually**	finally	circumstantially	possibly
7. **fundamental**	constructed	supposed	basic
8. **individual**	together	fellow	one person
9. **injury**	harm	assistance	illness
10. **obvious**	clear	terrible	potent
11. **possess**	purchase	trade	own
12. **responsibility**	action	respect	duty

C. **The word "animated" derives from a Greek word related to the idea of "breath" or "life." Each of the following sentences describes a word that is related to "animated." Match the correct words to the sentences and underline words or phrases in the sentence that helped you make your guess.**

a. *animal*	c. *animation*	e. *animise*	g. *animosity*	i. *inanimate*
b. *animate*	d. *anime*	f. *animism*	h. *animus*	j. *reanimate*

1. _____ Carol became a zoologist because she wanted to study the living creatures of the world.

2. _____ Many native cultures in the Americas, Asia, and Africa believe in spirits all around them.

3. _____ Dr. Frankenstein created the monster while trying to bring dead tissue back to life.

4. _____ All we have ever found on the moon are samples of lifeless objects, such as rocks and dust.

5. _____ Mary is so good with computers that she was able to create moving images that really look like they are alive.

6. _____ I think Terry is spending too much time watching Japanese shows that depict realistic sex and violence.

D. Choose from our vocabulary words to complete this Zuni myth about the Gods of War.[8]

One day the twin gods of war grew angry at the god of storms. You see the morning after a storm, the brothers wanted to go hunting, and they _____ (1) that their hunting ground would be just as they had left them with animals around and an easy hunt to be enjoyed. However, as they _____ (2) the hunting ground, they found the earth was soaking wet from the rains and their feet sunk into the mud making it impossible for them to hunt. It was clear who had ruined their fine day—the storm god. It was his _____ (3) to bring the rains. Only he owned the tools that made the heavens weep.

Now, the god of storms was a powerful god, and the brothers knew they could cause him no _____ (4), but in their awful mood, they would be happy enough if they could cause him insult. They thought and thought to hatch a plot, and at last an idea came to them. Oh, it was a grand idea! If there was one _____ (5) who could sneak into the palace of the storm god without being seen, it was their uncle, the centipede. Of course, in those times the centipede was as large as a man. But the brothers supposed that he could crawl undetected along the walls and ceiling to steal what they had asked for. The brothers pleaded with him, and _____ (6) the centipede's fear of the storm god, he finally agreed to do it.

Impatiently the gods of war waited and waited, until at last their uncle returned. As he came near, it was clear that he was carrying what they had asked for—the thunder stone and lightning shaft of the storm god! Now the brothers _____ (7) the tools they needed for their revenge. They climbed onto the roof of their house and beat the thunder stone and shook the lightning staff and the heavens became _____ (8) with a mighty storm. The rains fell so heavily that the land began to flood, but they did not care, for it is an _____ (9) of the gods of the war that they care not for the harm that they cause to others. They were simply alive with joy for the trouble they were causing.

But in their pleasure, they had forgotten something very important—their poor grandmother trapped in the house, trapped beneath the rising flood waters. When _____ (10) the boys concluded their game and the waters receded, they entered the house and found their grandmother had breathed her last. It was _____ (11) that the boys had succeeded in their desire to bring destruction, but they had failed in their duty to her. Where they buried her, the very first pepper bush grew, a plant with fruit that burned one's mouth, just as her heart burned with the betrayal of her grandsons. As for the centipede, he was punished by being shrunk to the size he is today.

E. Now circle synonyms for the following vocabulary words in the story above. You will find them in the paragraphs indicated by the numbers in parentheses.

a. possess **(1)**   **c.** eventually **(2)**   **e.** approach **(3)**   **g.** obvious **(3)**

b. assume **(2)**   **d.** animated **(3)**   **f.** injury **(3)**   **h.** responsibility **(4)**

MYTHOLOGY

Active reading can help you better understand a college text. Begin by discussing the questions below. Then carefully read the following essay, taking notes on the main points and important details, characters, and events that you find in the text. Also select the best meaning for words highlighted in the right-hand column.

PREREADING DISCUSSION

1. The Zuni are an ancient Native American nation. What do you know about them? What can you tell about any other Native American people?
2. The Zuni use stories about gods and spirits to teach their young about responsibilities they have. Can you think of any stories you learned when you were a child that helped you to understand your responsibilities?
3. What kind of character or behavior would you expect from an eagle, a coyote, or a turtle?

(1)   One of the unfortunate tendencies that people have when they consider the spiritual beliefs of others—beliefs that are foreign to them—is to assume that those beliefs are simply wrong. Consequently, when religious individuals talk about other cultures, they apply the term "myth" to describe the beliefs of those
5   cultures. In essence, my faith is a religion, while your faith is a cult, a sect. My stories of God are true, while the stories that you tell are myths about gods and spirits that simply do not exist. The purpose of mythology is not to study myths as fairy tales or as false beliefs. Rather, mythology provides an insight into culture and the stories that people around the world narrate to their children and
10   their children's children so that the young may grow to adulthood with a greater appreciation for the world around them and with an understanding of their responsibilities within that world.

> **line 4: apply**
>
> *a.*   to use
> *b.*   to seek employment
> *c.*   to be relevant
>
> **Another example:**
> *When our first method failed to improve the procedure, we applied a different method.*

(2)   Take the Zuni of New Mexico, for example. When anthropologist Frank Hamilton Cushing arrived
15   in Zuni Pueblo in 1879, he dedicated himself to learning about Zuni culture, and he quickly comprehended that to do so, he needed to understand their religion and their myths.[8] Cushing came to appreciate that the stories of Zuni gods and spirits
20   were not simply bedtime fables told to children or interesting tales told around the campfire to entertain people. On the contrary, Zuni myths are a means for conveying culture—for educating the people about their origins, their relationship to the earth, and the
25   duties they must fulfill for the wellbeing of the entire tribe and for the world around them.

Illustration of Zuni Pueblo below the Sacred Mountain

(3)   Like so many other Native American nations, the Zuni are principally animists, which means that they believe in an infinite number of spirits dwelling in the world around them. In the trees, the animals, the streams, even in the
30   apparently inanimate rocks there is an endless sea of spirit. It is a fundamental aspect of Zuni beliefs that life is all around us. And because we as humans affect so much of the world, we have the ability to do terrible harm not only to one another, but to those other lives in the natural world. The spirit of every tree we cut down feels the pain that we inflict. Every animal we cage or kill possesses a
35   spirit that suffers from our cruelty.   Therefore, every individual must strive to live in peace with the natural world.

(4)   One Zuni myth describes a young man of Zuni who possessed an eagle, which he kept in a cage. He loved the eagle so much that he would neglect his duties to his family, leaving the farm in the hands of his brothers, while he would 40   spend all day beside the cage, admiring his bird. His brothers became so angry at the young man's obvious obsession that they plotted to kill the eagle. Early the next morning, when no one else was around, the eagle spoke up, exposing the plot to the young man and pleading with him to set her free. He agreed to do so, but only if she would take him with her wherever she went.

45   (5)   And so they flew away together, the mighty eagle carrying the young man aloft into the sky until, far from his native home, she set him in a tree and landed on a branch beside him. Then she transformed into a beautiful young woman to sit and speak with him further. Upon sight of her in this form, his obsession grew swiftly into affection. He declared his love for her and swore to 50   stay with her for all time, even though he could not fly. She gave him her heart and helped him stitch together a special set of wings with which he learned to fly.

(6)   With time, even her own family of eagles came to accept him, although there was always suspicion of this strange man who had turned his back on his own family. The eagle maiden too was worried, fearful that his eyes might stray 55   to the land of death beyond their borders. One day while floating in the sky, he saw people below him—beautiful smiling people calling to him from a land not far away. The eagle maiden warned him about this dangerous land, and he gave her his word to follow her guidance. Nevertheless, he joined a celebration with them—despite her warnings—and was forever cursed by the touch of death.

60   (7)   The young man returned to the eagles, his own eagle wings torn, and he begged for the maiden's forgiveness, but she could no longer trust him. He had caused too much injury to her and her people, and the eagles commanded her to take him back to his own people. Quickly she grabbed him in her talons and flew away with him as tears of pain and anger filled her eyes. However, just as they 65   approached his village from the sky, her heart trembled with so much fury that she opened her talons and released him. From high above he fell, the young man who had ignored his responsibilities and neglected his family. He fell and fell and at last crashed into the earth and died.

(8)   Many myths of the Zuni demonstrate how the creatures of the world are 70   more than just animated—they have voice and character. And if they have personalities, then they can behave in ways that we as humans should recognize as good and bad. Again, the point of such stories is not just to entertain, but to teach. Zuni children learn from the eagle maiden story about responsibility and dedication to family and commitment to keeping one's word. However, in some 75   myths, it is the animals who misbehave, and in their misbehavior there are more lessons to learn.

(9)   In the old days, a turtle once set a trap that killed a deer and he was anxious to eat the animal's meat, but he lacked the sharp claws and teeth or even a knife with which he could cut the deer open. As he sat complaining about this 80   and how hungry he was, a coyote overheard him. The cunning coyote approached the turtle and offered to help for a share of the food. The turtle agreed. However, when the coyote had finished cutting up the deer, the turtle only offered him the deer's stomach and liver, keeping all the best parts of the deer for himself. The coyote became furious and tried to attack the turtle, but the

---

line 52: come

a.   to approach
b.   to happen
c.   to proceed

Another example:
After a couple months, I came to realize that I needed to work harder if I really wanted to learn English well.

---

line 74: word

a.   promise
b.   conversation
c.   term

Another example:
I just don't think Teresa will ever keep her word about staying away from cigarettes.

85   turtle simply hid within his shell—where the coyote could cause him no injury—
and waited.

(10)   Eventually, the coyote gave up and went away to gather his family to
help him take the meat away, but while he was gone, the turtle dragged the meat
high into a tree, too high for the coyote to reach it. When the coyote returned
90   with his wife and children, he realized he had again been tricked and howled for
the meat. He knew the turtle would have to come down eventually, and he
vowed to destroy him the moment he did. The turtle had to think quickly now
and he devised a cunning plan. He called to the coyotes to approach the tree and
he, the turtle, would throw the delicious soft meat down to them. Yet the
95   moment the coyotes were close enough, the turtle threw down instead the heavy
bones, which crushed the coyotes beneath their weight.

(11)   Now to the outsider, it must seem obvious that these are simply
fantasies—stories that have no relation to reality. How could anyone believe that
a turtle could kill a deer and climb a tree? And yet you do not have to believe
100   that a turtle can accomplish such incredible acts; what matters is that you can
learn from the ingenuity of the turtle how to use your own intelligence to
overcome great challenges, despite your size or physical weakness. You can also
learn from such Zuni myths where peppers come from, why coyote has whiskers,
and even why a beetle keeps its head to the ground as it walks along.

105   (12)   Of course, a beetle is even smaller and weaker than a turtle, especially
compared to a coyote. Still, even the lowly beetle should be able to defeat the
coyote—not through physical strength, but through intelligence. The Zuni say
that a beetle was passing over the land when a coyote approached, and hungry for
a small snack, the coyote threatened to consume the beetle. The beetle knew it
110   could not outrun the coyote, nor could it overpower him. So it thought quickly
and lowered its head to the ground. Just as the coyote leaned down to snap it up
into his jaws, the beetle declared, "Wait! Wait a moment, my friend! Listen!
Don't you hear that?"

(13)   The coyote looked suspiciously at the beetle. "I don't hear
115   anything," he said.

"Wait!" shouted the beetle. "There it is again!"

"What?"

"Voices," the beetle explained. "The spirits of the earth."

The coyote's eyes grew wide with fear. "Wh-what are they saying?"

120   "Oh dear," the beetle sighed. "The spirits are not happy. They say that
certain animals have been passing over the land and freely using the land as their
own toilet! Can you believe that? For shame!"

(14)   The coyote remembered how just that morning, passing through this
very area, he had gone to the bathroom behind a nearby tree. "Oh no!" he said.

125   "Oh yes!" said the beetle. "And the spirits are so angry that they will
soon rise up from the ground and punish any creature they find who has
committed such a terrible act."

And with that, the coyote turned tail and ran away as swiftly as possible.

---

line 100: **matter**

a.   material
b.   issue
c.   be important

Another example:
*Do you think it matters
what day we choose for
our party?*

---

line 127: **commit**

a.   to imprison
b.   to promise
c.   to do

Another example:
*In 1936, Kim Hanson was
put in prison for
commiting murder.*

MYTHOLOGY

A. *Which of the following statements best expresses the main point that the writer of "Man and the Spirits of Zuni" is trying to make?*

1. Cultures around the world possess myths, which are stories about gods and spirits and how they interact with humans.

2. Myths are not just stories that entertain people, but a way of teaching people about themselves, their responsibilities, and their connection to the world around them.

3. The Zuni of New Mexico are talented myth-makers, telling stories about how animals can talk with humans and behave in ways that are good and bad.

B. *Read the following statements. Do they agree with the information in the essay? Circle T (true) or F (false) for each statement.*

1. T   F   Only one culture has true religion while other cultures have myths.
2. T   F   Frank Hamilton Cushing was a zoologist.
3. T   F   Cushing studied the myths of the people of Zuni.
4. T   F   The Zuni are a native culture from South America.
5. T   F   Animism is based on the belief that there is only one god.
6. T   F   The purpose of Zuni myths is to teach children how to profit from the world.

C. *Match the following lessons or origins with the stories told by the Zuni. There may be more than one correct answer.*

>   *(a) Eagle Maiden*   *(b) Coyote and Turtle*   *(c) Coyote and Beetle*   *(d) Gods of War*

1. _____ Intelligence matters more than strength.
2. _____ Where hot peppers come from.
3. _____ A man's first duty is to his family.
4. _____ Keep your head down and stay alive.
5. _____ Why centipedes are so small.
6. _____ Why the sky growls with thunder.
7. _____ If a man flies too high, he may fall to his death.
8. _____ A man's place is with his own people.
9. _____ Never steal from the gods.
10. _____ A creature with wings is meant to fly free.

D. Look at the underlined transition words in each of the following passages from the essay "Man and the Spirits of Zuni." Circle the letter of the word or phrase that comes closest to expressing the same meaning as the transition word within the context of that passage.

1. One of the unfortunate tendencies that people have…is to assume that those beliefs are simply wrong. <u>Consequently</u>, when religious individuals talk about other cultures, they apply the term "myth" to describe the beliefs of those cultures. *(lines 1–5)*

    a. *subsequently*   b. *however*   c. *as a result*

2. The purpose of mythology is not to study myths as fairy tales or as false beliefs. <u>Rather</u>, mythology provides an insight into culture and the stories that people around the world narrate to their children and their children's children. *(lines 7–10)*

    a. *instead*   b. *on the other hand*   c. *preferably*

3. Cushing came to appreciate that the stories of Zuni gods and spirits were not simply bedtime fables told to children or interesting tales told around the campfire to entertain people. <u>On the contrary</u>, Zuni myths are a means for conveying culture. *(lines 18–23)*

    a. *in fact*   b. *but*   c. *opposite*

4. <u>Like</u> so many other Native American nations, the Zuni are principally animists, which means that they believe in an infinite number of spirits dwelling in the world around them. *(lines 27–29)*

    a. *enjoying*   b. *as with*   c. *you might say*

5. Every animal we cage or kill possesses a spirit that suffers from our cruelty. <u>Therefore</u>, every individual must strive to live in peace with the natural world. *(lines 34–36)*

    a. *thus*   b. *at that time*   c. *for instance*

6. He declared his love for her and swore to stay with her for all time, <u>even though</u> he could not fly. *(lines 49–50)*

    a. *however*   b. *although*   c. *because*

7. The eagle maiden warned him about this dangerous land, and he gave her his word to follow her guidance. <u>Nevertheless</u>, he joined a celebration with them—despite her warnings—and was forever cursed by the touch of death. *(lines 57–59)*

    a. *still*   b. *not ever*   c. *fortunately*

8. Zuni children learn from the eagle maiden story about responsibility and dedication to family and commitment to keeping one's word. <u>However</u>, in some myths, it is the animals who misbehave, and in their misbehavior there are more lessons to learn. *(lines 73–76)*

    a. *indeed*   b. *nevertheless*   c. *yet*

9. He called to the coyotes to approach the tree and he, the turtle, would throw the delicious soft meat down to them. <u>Yet</u> the moment the coyotes were close enough, the turtle threw down instead the heavy bones, which crushed the coyotes beneath their weight. *(lines 93–96)*

    a. *still not*   b. *but*   c. *just*

10. The beetle knew it could not outrun the coyote, nor could it overpower him. <u>So</u> it thought quickly and lowered its head to the ground. *(lines 109–11)*

    a. *therefore*   b. *very*   c. *like*

MYTHOLOGY

A. CONTRAST MARKERS AND HOW THEY ARE USED

Contrast markers are adverbs that connect ideas or clauses in which there is a contrast or opposition. These two ideas might be directly opposite each other in meaning, or it may be that both ideas are true, even though you would not expect them to be true because they seem to be opposite. For example:

DIRECT OPPOSITION: *I was born in California, but I live in New Jersey.*

There is nothing surprising about someone being born in one state and moving to another state later on. It happens frequently. Direct opposition contrast markers are used to show this obviously contrary relationship, and you learn these markers very early in learning English, for example:

but	**however**	**on the other hand**	**while**	**whereas**

UNEXPECTED OPPOSITION: *I live in New Jersey even though I work in Virginia.*

It is strange that someone would live in one state, but work in a state that is not directly nearby. This is an unexpected situation. In literature, stories, and myths unexpected things happen. That's why we enjoy reading or listening to such stories. We can still use simple contrast markers for these situations, but there are a few special contrast markers for unexpected situations:

although	*even though*	*though*	*nonetheless*	*nevertheless*
still	*yet*	*however*	*despite*	*in spite of*

B. Circle the contrast markers in the following passages from the essay "Man and the Spirits of Zuni." Then underline and number (1) and (2) the two ideas that are being contrasted.

1. Cushing came to appreciate that the stories of Zuni gods and spirits were not simply bedtime fables told to children or interesting tales told around the campfire to entertain people. On the contrary, Zuni myths are a means for conveying culture. *(lines 16–20)*

2. He agreed to do so, but only if she would take him with her wherever she went. *(lines 41–42)*

3. He declared his love for her and swore to stay with her for all time, even though he could not fly. *(lines 47–48)*

4. With time, even her own family of eagles came to accept him, although there was always suspicion of this strange man who had turned his back on his own family. *(lines 50–52)*

5. He gave her his word to follow her guidance. Nevertheless, he joined a celebration with them—despite her warnings—and was forever cursed by the touch of death. *(lines 55–57)*

6. He called to the coyotes to approach the tree and he, the turtle, would throw the delicious soft meat down to them. Yet the moment the coyotes were close enough, the turtle threw down instead the heavy bones, which crushed the coyotes beneath their weight. *(lines 91–94)*

7. A beetle is even smaller and weaker than a turtle, especially compared to a coyote. Still, even the lowly beetle should be able to defeat the coyote—not through physical strength, but through intelligence. *(lines 103–05)*

C. *Circle the letter of the best option to complete the texts below and ensure that you have expressed an unexpected contrast.*

1. Although Heinrich Schliemann had no real training in professional archaeology, ...

   a. he made many terrible mistakes in the field.

   b. he became one of the most famous archaeologists of all time.

2. Most people in the United States do not belong to Native American cultures.

   a. However, they have no reason to study Native American myths.

   b. However, they can benefit from studying Native American myths.

3. The pharaohs of ancient Egypt were just men.

   a. Still, the people of Egypt treated the pharaohs like gods.

   b. Still, the pharaohs died just like everyone else.

4. Even though Ivan Pavlov was not a psychologist, ...

   a. students majoring in Psychology are required to know about his research.

   b. students majoring in Psychology spend more time studying Sigmund Freud.

5. Frank Hamilton Cushing eventually became a shaman among the Zuni ...

   a. despite the fact that he was an outsider with no connections to the tribe.

   b. despite the fact that he learned and adopted Zuni culture as his own.

6. Many people wanted George Washington to stay in power in the United States government.

   a. Nevertheless, Washington served his full term as president.

   b. Nevertheless, Washington resigned at the end of his term as president.

D. *Write your own sentences with unexpected contrasts.*

1. Although I _____, my
   family _____

2. My home country _____.
   Nevertheless, I feel _____

3. Many people love _____.
   However, I _____

4. Despite how expensive it is, I still _____
   _____

5. My best friend _____, but I
   _____

MYTHOLOGY

Choose from the following options for your journal writing assignment:

1.   One of the central issues that comes up in Zuni myths is the relationship between humans and the earth, including our ties with other people and animals and the environment itself. The Zuni believed that we as individuals can become quite ill and possibly die if we lose harmony between ourselves and the world of nature. What do you think about this idea? What does the world mean to you? How would you describe your relationship to the natural world? Can you identify things that you do that actually help or harm the world around you? Complete the following table with examples of what you do to the world around you. Then write about these things.

how I help the world	how I harm the world

2.   In English-speaking countries, it is quite common that children learn about myths as they go through school, perhaps as kids, and even more so later as adults. Classical mythology has long been a favorite interest for western cultures—the myths of ancient Greece and Rome. Have you ever read classical myths? Are you familiar with myths or tales from other cultures, such as your home culture? Do you know any myths well enough to actually tell them? Write two or three myths in your journal.

3.   For this writing assignment, I'd like you to write your own myth or fable, something along the lines that we have seen with the Zuni—a story about animals. Or about humans and animals. Let's start by thinking imaginatively about what kind of characters animals could be in your story. Write a list of five animals along with a proper name and a brief description for each one. For example, if you chose to include a wolf in your story, perhaps you could call him "Bora," and you might describe him as "strong, gray, and very hungry." Once you have finished your list, compose your story.

  Animal   **Name**   **Description**

1. _____

2. _____

3. _____

4. _____

5. _____

MYTHOLOGY

A. *Here are our target vocabulary for Reading 2 in this unit. Draw a line to match each vocabulary word to the most appropriate definition.*

1.	achieve	**a.**	To take something by force or legal authority.
2.	community	**b.**	A very sad or shocking event.
3.	decline	**c.**	To succeed in doing something.
4.	derive	**d.**	A territory controlled by a king.
5.	domain	**e.**	Moving to a new place for work or residence.
6.	dwell	**f.**	Having a resemblance to someone or something.
7.	embrace	**g.**	To deteriorate in power or go down in quality.
8.	migration	**h.**	To live in a location or home.
9.	seize	**i.**	To hold someone or believe in something.
10.	similar	**j.**	A job or duty assigned to someone to accomplish.
11.	task	**k.**	A group of people who live in the same location.
12.	tragedy	**l.**	To stem from a source or origin.

B. *Write the letter of the correct synonym to match the meaning of the vocabulary words highlighted in the sentences below.*

1. _____ I offered to help Teresa with her homework, but she **declined**. She said she had to learn how to do it on her own.

   a. *descend*

   b. *decrease*

2. _____ To reach my house, go half a mile on Main Street, and then just before the road **declines**, turn right.

   c. *refuse*

   d. *fall*

3. _____ Our funds have **declined** so much that I doubt we can afford to finish this project on time—if ever!

   e. *shrink*

4. _____ Our researchers have been **tasked** with studying the effects of caffeine on a worker's ability to concentrate.

   f. *chore*

   g. *nuisance*

5. _____ Since I moved out of my parents' house, I understand just how time-consuming all these daily **tasks** are at home.

   h. *mission*

   i. *assignment*

6. _____ I used to enjoy gardening, but now it is such a **task** to pull the weeds and water the plants. I just want to stop sometimes.

   j. *appoint*

C. *Below are excerpts from the essay we will read in this chapter, "Love and Tragedy of the Celts." Vocabulary words have been highlighted in the texts, but there are also synonyms in each excerpt. Circle the synonyms you find.*

1. And yet a contemporary culture to the classical Greeks has been largely ignored over the years, despite its own rich heritage and despite the fact that they share a comparable origin with the Greeks. You see, it is quite likely that the ancient Celts followed a **similar** path to that of the Greeks. *(lines 2–5)*

2. Celtic **communities** had their own languages from the British Isles in the north to Spain and even Egypt in the south, and from France in the west to Turkey in the east. Most of the languages of those societies have died out, but a few survive even today. *(lines 16–19)*

3. The Celts **embraced** their own religion, holding a unique sense of spirituality and a reverence for their own gods and myths and heroes. *(lines 26–27)*

4. Strangers **migrated** from over the seas. Celtic settlers from far away Spain relocated to the islands. *(lines 68–69)*

5. Emer, his wife, would not give herself to the young warrior unless he proved himself; he had to **achieve** a series of superhuman tasks reminiscent of Hercules. Yet Cuchulainn accomplished each one, even staying awake an entire year just to show her how much he loved her. *(lines 80–83)*

6. He sent Fergus MacRo and his three sons to convey the king's pardon and to invite them back to his **domain** for a great feast. However, when MacRo and his sons reached the home in Scotland and saw fair Deirdre and the beauty of her love for Naois, they swore to protect them if they decided to return to the king's realm in Ulster. *(lines 103–07)*

D. *Certain words, such as prepositions, often go together with particular nouns, adjectives, or verbs. These combinations are known as collocations. Complete these sentences with the correct prepositions from the list below. If no preposition is needed, then write an "X" in the space provided.*

of	to	by	from	at	over	in

1. Last year I joined a **community** _____ writers and artists near Santa Fe, New Mexico.

2. The Mbuti pygmies of the Democratic Republic of Congo are a nomadic people who **dwell** _____ temporary shelters made of trees and leaves.

3. Although cultures around the world may seem very different, in many ways they are actually quite **similar** _____ one another.

4. When Marianne arrived at the airport, her mother quickly **embraced** _____ her.

5. I was given the **task** _____ organizing all our receipts by month of purchase.

6. Nobu is determined to **achieve** _____ his goals before the end of the year.

7. Many people don't realize this, but the English language **derives** _____ German.

8. When he lost his job, the bank **seized** _____ Martin's house.

MYTHOLOGY

Discuss the questions below with your peers. Then carefully read the following essay, taking notes on the main points and important details, characters, and events that you find in the text. Also select the best meaning for words highlighted in the right-hand column.

PREREADING DISCUSSION

1. Who were the earliest European cultures? What ancient western civilizations are you familiar with? Can you describe them?
2. Who were the Celts? Have you heard of them before? Where did they live?
3. Love and romance are very popular themes in art and literature. Do you know any myths about love? Can you describe any famous lovers in the stories and myths of your own home culture?

(1)   Students in US American colleges are no doubt familiar with Greek and Roman myths. And yet a contemporary culture to the classical Greeks has been largely ignored over the years, despite its own rich heritage and despite the fact that they share a comparable origin with the Greeks. You see, it is quite likely
5   that the ancient Celts[9] followed a similar path to that of the Greeks—deriving from somewhere in eastern Europe before migrating south and west into the very lands where they still dwell today, although under very different names.

(2)   Human history is truly the long and volatile history of migrations, with large powerful nations often stemming from very humble beginnings indeed in
10   far off corners of the globe. And as they were journeying from east to west, the Celts no doubt learned from and adapted to their new environments. In fact, while they had become semi-literate in the early centuries following the birth of Christ with the invention of the Celtic *Ogham* script, the Celts lacked a popular fully formed script of their own until they adopted the Latin alphabet that you
15   are reading now.

(3)   Likewise, Celtic communities had their own languages from the British Isles in the north to Spain and even Egypt in the south, and from France in the west to Turkey in the east. Most of the languages of those societies have died out, but a few survive even today, although most descendants of the Celts never
20   learn them. Instead, they communicate in English, French, or German, just to name a few of the languages that emerged in the once extensive regions of Celtic civilization. The notable exceptions to this decline are in Ireland and Wales especially, where children in school are required to learn something of the old language, and to a lesser extent in Scotland, Cornwall, the Isle of Man,
25   and Brittany.

(4)   Finally, the Celts embraced their own religion, holding a unique sense of spirituality and a reverence for their own gods and myths and heroes. And yet most Celts eventually abandoned their religion in favor of Christianity. However, it is to this ancient religion and its related body of myths that we now
30   turn our attention, beginning with the polytheistic nature of Celtic belief. Like the Greeks and Egyptians of old, the Celts believed in hundreds of gods, although in contrast to the Greeks and Egyptians, who kept extensive written records of their beliefs and practices, the Celts depended more on an oral tradition. This naturally makes it more difficult for modern researchers to know exactly what the
35   Celts believed and how they worshipped, but we do have enough information to relate the following tales.

line 6: very

a.   much
b.   actual
c.   simple

Another example:
I'm glad you're here, Bob. You're the very man I was looking for.

A Celtic Christian cross

line 21: once

a.   one time
b.   ever
c.   formerly

Another example:
The Celts were once a mighty civilization.

(5)   The gods of Celtic Britain—and eventually the people themselves—
were descended from two divine couples: Beli and Don on the one hand, and
Bran and Llyr on the other. Now these two families were deeply divided,
40   distrusting one another to the point of engaging in open war more than on just
one occasion. Yet it was the descendants of these two couples who would
populate the tales told by the Celts of Britain, tales full of love and longing and
honor, but also stories of betrayal and magic and witches.

(6)   In Ireland, the mother goddess Don became Danu, and it was said that
45   the children of Danu were a beautiful god-like people with flowing golden hair
who descended from the heavens on clouds to dwell on the earth. They were the
Tuatha de Danann—the children of the mother goddess, and their king was
Dagda. Now Dagda was known to be a good king, a lover of knowledge and of
women and of food. It was said that he kept a great cauldron with him, so huge it
50   required its own transport whenever the king traveled. However, it was worth
the effort to move it, because even while people were eating, the great Cauldron
of Dagda never ceased to produce more food for those in need.

(7)   However, the descendants of Danu could not
overcome the children of Bran and Llyr, their rivals. In the
55   end, Dagda had no choice but to guide his people to a new
domain underground, leaving the world above to their
enemies. To offer the Children of Danu the finest home,
Dagda had barrows or mounds built for them. His own home
was the mound of Newgrange, which archaeologists later
60   excavated and discovered to have been constructed around
3200 BC, the same time that ancient Egyptians were learning
how to write hieroglyphics. There is still disagreement
among experts about the purpose of the mound, but Celtic
myths explained that Dagda was tricked out of his home at
65   Newgrange by his own son. Even while the power of Dagda
was declining, the Children of Danu were learning to survive
in the lands below, evolving over time to become the fairy
folk, including the banshees and leprechauns.

The mound of Newgrange in Ireland

(8)   As time passed, the lands above fell into new hands. Strangers migrated
70   from over the seas. Celtic settlers from far away Spain relocated to the islands
and joined with the Celtic Irish race who spread over the island and even across
the water into Britain, taking their language and myths with them. Myths tell that
the people below ground continued to mingle from time to time with those above
ground, and even fell in love. From one such affair was born Cuchulainn, the
75   greatest of the ancient Irish heroes and son of Lugh, God of the Sun. From early
on it was clear that Cuchulainn was different from other men. He possessed a
strength that was beyond human and a wild frenzy in battle that frightened both
friend and foe. It was also clear that tragedy followed him all his days.

(9)   Women were drawn to Cuchulainn, yet sometimes they suffered for their
80   love. Emer, his wife, would not give herself to the young warrior unless he
proved himself; he had to achieve a series of superhuman tasks reminiscent of
Hercules. Yet Cuchulainn accomplished each one, even staying awake an entire
year just to show her how much he loved her. However, after they were married,
his eyes quickly strayed to other women, including Aoife, who became pregnant
85   from Cuchulainn. The hero did not know about this until 15 years later when a

| line 38: **divine** |
| *a.* holy |
| *b.* lovely |
| *c.* prophesy |
| **Another example:** |
| *Many cultures believe in a divine being who created the world.* |

| line 74: **affair** |
| *a.* relationship |
| *b.* business |
| *c.* party |
| **Another example:** |
| *Martha and Miguel could not keep their affair secret for long.* |

young man named Connla arrived in Ulster and challenged Cuchulainn to battle. Cuchulainn defeated the stranger, killing him with his javelin. Only afterwards did he notice the ring on Connla's finger—the same ring that Cuchulainn had given to Aoife 15 years earlier.

90   **(10)**   Perhaps the greatest of tragic love stories in Celtic lore is that of Deirdre and Naois. There once was a king of Ulster named Connacher, and he had heard of a maiden said to be so beautiful that Connacher had to see for himself if the stories were true. So he traveled with his soldiers to the land of this maiden, where he found her home in the forest. As he was looking at her, he realized that
95   she was indeed the fairest woman he had ever seen. And he knew he had to have her. So he seized her and brought her back to his castle to wed him, but Deirdre pleaded that she be allowed a year and a day respite, and at the end of that time, she would marry him. King Connacher agreed.

    (11)   Time passed, and one day while she was roaming the fields of Ulster,
100 Deirdre saw a young man named Naois, who was traveling with his two brothers Allen and Arden. Naois and Deirdre embraced and fell in love, but fearful of the king's wrath, they traveled north into Scotland, there to dwell in safety and joy. But the king discovered their hiding place and set a trap. He sent Fergus MacRo and his three sons to convey the king's pardon and to invite them back to his
105 domain for a great feast. However, when MacRo and his sons reached the home in Scotland and saw fair Deirdre and the beauty of her love for Naois, they swore to protect them if they decided to return to the king's realm in Ulster.

    (12)   And so they traveled to Ulster, and Connacher sent out 300 warriors to kill Naois and his brothers, but the sons of MacRo stood between them and
110 would not let through a single warrior. When all the warriors lay dead on the field, Naois and Deirdre knew then that they could not trust the promises of the king, so the lovers fled with Allen and Arden, journeying back to Scotland. Connacher, desperate and enraged, called on his mighty druid to use magic to stop them from escaping. The druid caused the grassy plain to flood with a
115 gray and shallow sea, and turned the waters into stones as sharp as swords and as poisonous as snakes.

    (13)   Arden was the first to fall, and Naois grabbed him and placed his lifeless body on his own shoulder beside Deirdre. But then Allen too succumbed to the blades and the poison, and as he breathed his last, Naois lifted
120 him onto his other shoulder. And even as the poison coursed through his own blood, Naois would not stop. He refused to leave his beloved in the midst of such mortal danger. So he continued on until he reached Scotland and the shores of Loch Ness, and there he collapsed and perished.

    (14)   A wide grave was dug for the three brothers, and as she was standing
125 beside the open grave, Deirdre said to her beloved Naois, "If the dead had any sense to feel, Ye would have made a place for Deirdre." At her lament, the bodies did indeed move aside, making a place for her, and so she lay down beside Naois and died. However, King Connacher in his jealousy had the grave dug up and the bodies of the brothers moved to the other side of the lake. But
130 even then, a fir tree grew from the grave of Naois and another fir tree grew from the grave of Deirdre, and a shoot from each tree grew over the lake and twined together. And each time Connacher tried to cut down the shoots, they again grew out and embraced one another over the gentle loch.

*The Giant's Causeway
in Ireland*

---

line 117: fall

a.   *collapse*
b.   *fail*
c.   *die*

Another example:
*Despite his great
strength, the king
eventually fell in battle.*

MYTHOLOGY

A. Quickly scan through the first few paragraphs of the essay to find the names of ten different countries or cultures and write them below.

1. _____

2. _____

3. _____

4. _____

5. _____

6. _____

7. _____

8. _____

9. _____

10. _____

B. Draw lines to link the following names from Celtic mythology with an appropriate description.

1. Aoife   **a.** The first to die among the poisoned rocks.

2. Arden   **b.** Her son was killed by her son's own father.

3. Connacher   **c.** Frightened both friends and enemies in battle.

4. Connla   **d.** Was worshipped as the mother goddess.

5. Cuchulainn   **e.** Protected two young lovers against the king's army.

6. Dagda   **f.** Died in battle against his own father.

7. Danu   **g.** Mother of the *Tuatha de Danann*.

8. Deirdre   **h.** Laid down to die in the grave of her lover.

9. Don   **i.** Father of the greatest hero in Irish mythology.

10. Emer   **j.** Died trying to save his brothers and his lover.

11. Lugh   **k.** Made homes for his people in mounds.

12. MacRo   **l.** Used a druid to kill his rival.

13. Naois   **m.** Challenged her lover to stay awake for one year.

14. Ulster   **n.** The kingdom of Connacher.

C. *Circle the letter of the best option to complete the sentences below based on your reading of the essay.*

1. The Celtic cultures of
    Europe _____

    a. were very similar to ancient Greek and Roman cultures
    b. probably originated from the same part of Europe as the Greeks
    c. worshipped the same gods as did the ancient Egyptians

2. The Celtic people invented
    the _____

    a. Ogham script
    b. Latin script
    c. hieroglyphic script

3. Celtic civilization existed in
    _____, _____, and _____

    a. China
    b. Egypt
    c. Kenya
    d. Ireland
    e. Turkey
    f. Russia

4. The *Tuatha de Danann*
    were the descendants of
    _____

    a. Llyr
    b. Deirdre
    c. Danu

5. The Cauldron of Dagda was
    used to _____

    a. boil his enemies alive
    b. provide an endless supply of food
    c. store all of his wealth in gold

6. After they moved
    underground, the *Tuatha de
    Danann* became _____,
    _____, and _____

    a. trolls
    b. fairies
    c. wizards
    d. leprechauns
    e. demons
    f. banshees

7. Newgrange in Ireland was
    _____, _____, and _____

    a. the ancient home of the god Dagda
    b. built by the fairies for their king
    c. stolen away from the king by his son
    d. built around 5,000 years ago
    e. a burial mound for a powerful king
    f. excavated by Heinrich Schliemann

8. Cuchulainn differed from
    other men, because he was
    _____

    a. more intelligent
    b. more fierce
    c. more handsome

9. Cuchulainn unknowingly
    killed his own _____

    a. son
    b. father
    c. wife

10. King Connacher sought out
    Deirdre because of what he
    had heard about her _____

    a. wisdom
    b. wealth
    c. beauty

11. Naois carried _____, _____,
    and _____ over the
    poisonous stones.

    a. Don
    b. Dagda
    c. Deirdre
    d. Arden
    e. Allen
    f. Connacher

MYTHOLOGY

A. *THE STRUCTURE AND MEANING OF PAST TENSE VERBS*

There are several verb tenses in English that are used to describe past time, just as there are several tenses for present time and for future time. For example, can you identify the following verb tenses?

I did my homework last night.	→ _____	Tense
I had done my homework last night.	→ _____	Tense
I was doing my homework last night.	→ _____	Tense

Each tense indicates an aspect of the verb in that time that makes it different from other tenses. Recall how in Unit 1 we considered the Past Perfect Tense. Both the Simple Past and Past Perfect Tenses describe past time, but the Past Perfect Tense form tells us that one event happened before another event in the past.

I had finished doing my homework before I fell asleep last night. →

"I had finished doing my homework" first, and after that *"I fell asleep."*

Likewise, a verb in the Past Progressive Tense tells us that there is a special relationship between that verb or event and another event, for example, in the Simple Past Tense. In this case, however, it is not that one event happened before another event. Rather, Past Progressive Tense tells us that two events happened at the same time in the past.

While I was doing my homework last night, I began to fall asleep. →

While I was still doing my homework, I became very tired and started to fall asleep.

Unlike other verb tenses, such as the Simple Past Tense, the Past Progressive Tense can never be used alone or out of context. It is always used to show at least two separate events happening at the same time. These two events could have the following relationships with these associated tenses:

1. **Past Progressive Tense** *and* **Simple Past Tense** →

    One event began first and then the other event happened while the first event was still going on.

    For example, "While I was watching TV last night, my father called me."

2. **Past Progressive Tense** *and* **Past Progressive Tense** →

    Both events began at some point in the past and they were still in progress at the same time.

    For example, "While I was watching TV last night, I was also doing my homework."

3. **Past Progressive Tense** *and an unspecified* **past event** →

    One event began first and then the other event happened although the second event may not be specified.

    For example, the phone rings and William answers it:

    William: "Hello?"
    Michelle: "Hi, William."
    William: "Michelle? Hi! I was just watching TV. What are you doing?" [The phone call is the unspecified event that occurred while William was watching TV.]

B. Look at the sentences below. Underline the past tense verbs in the sentences. Write a, b, or c to indicate which relationship the verb in the past progressive tense has to other events in the sentence.

> **a) past progressive tense and simple past tense,**
> **b) past progressive tense and past progressive tense, or**
> **c) past progressive tense and an unspecified past event.**

1. _____ You know, I was just thinking, perhaps we should spend this weekend studying instead of going camping up in the canyon. We've got a big test coming up.

2. _____ Teresa heard a knock on the door. She was waiting for Mark to come by, but Mark never knocked on the door quite that hard. It had to be somebody else. But who?

3. _____ Emperor Constantine was waiting for the battle to begin when he saw a mystical light in the morning sky—a symbol, like a cross.

4. _____ While I was shopping this morning, I was thinking about how nice it would be to invite your parents over for dinner. What do you think? I bought a nice salmon.

5. _____ I never thought Cary would be caught. He always got away with his crimes. But when Cary arrived home late last night, two police officers were waiting for him at his door.

6. _____ The party was dull. That is, until I saw her. As our eyes met, I was thinking, 'Whatever else happens tonight, I need to find out this woman's name.'

7. _____ There's never a dull moment in our flat. When I got home after school, Paul was trying to eat ten huge pancakes while Celine was painting pictures of pancakes on the walls.

C. Look at these sentences from our reading. In each sentence, circle the verb in the Past Progressive Tense. Then underline the event that happened while that verb was in progress.

1. And as they were journeying from east to west, the Celts no doubt learned from and adapted to their new environments. *(lines 10–12)*

2. However, it was worth the effort to move it, because even while people were eating, the great Cauldron of Dagda never ceased to produce more food for those in need. *(lines 50–52)*

3. His own home was the mound of Newgrange, which archaeologists later excavated and discovered to have been constructed around 3200 BC, the same time that ancient Egyptians were learning how to write hieroglyphics. *(lines 58–62)*

4. As he was looking at her, he realized that she was indeed the fairest woman he had ever seen. *(lines 94–95)*

5. Time passed, and one day while she was roaming the fields of Ulster, Deirdre saw a young man named Naois, who was traveling with his two brothers Allen and Arden. *(lines 99–101)*

6. A wide grave was dug for the three brothers, and as she was standing beside the open grave, Deirdre said to her beloved Naois, "If the dead had any sense to feel, Ye would have made a place for Deirdre." *(lines 124–26)*

D. Complete the following sentences by circling the correct tenses of the verbs in italics.

1. Hey, John, I *head / am heading / headed* over to the Student Center to pick up some lunch. Would you like anything to eat?

2. Hercules *is shooting / shot / was shooting* arrows at the terrible Nemean Lion, when he realized that no arrow could actually pierce the lion's golden fur.

3. While he *is waiting / was waiting / waited* for Samantha to get home from work, Charles decided to clean the apartment from top to bottom.

4. On the flight from London to Paris, Laya *thought / was thinking / is thinking* a lot about where she should go first: the Louvre Museum, the Eiffel Tower, or perhaps the Arc de Triomphe.

5. Miss McDougal *is waiting / waits / was waiting* outside to see you, Mrs. Thomas. Should I show her in?

6. One thing I *know / knew / was knowing* the moment that I saw you at the café sipping your drink and watching the people go by—this man knows how to relax and have a good time.

7. I'm so glad you're here, Martin. I *am wondering / wonder / was wondering* if you would come, and I could really use your help moving this furniture.

8. Nora *writes / was writing / is writing* her paper for her history class while I was getting dinner ready, but we both really just wanted to go out to eat that night.

E. Complete the following sentences with your own ideas. Each sentence should include a verb in the Past Progressive Tense to indicate two events happening at the same time.

1. I was still living back in my home country when _____

   _____

2. I remember when I heard about the attacks of 9/11 in the United States, I was _____

   _____

3. While I was sleeping last night, _____

   _____

4. When aliens landed outside my house, I _____

   _____

5. I got a call from the president as I _____

   _____

6. I was _____

   when suddenly the earth began to shake and my father screamed.

7. As the Titanic was sailing out to sea, I knew that _____

   _____

MYTHOLOGY

Choose from the following options for your journal writing assignment:

1. Certain civilizations, such as the Greeks and Romans, are often studied in school because people believe that these civilizations did something important—that they made a lasting contribution to our society or even to the world around us. However, people may be less familiar with the contributions and advances made by other cultures, especially distant cultures. Use your own knowledge, your peers, a library, or the Internet to complete the following chart with three different cultures and at least three contributions, inventions, or advances made by each one. When you have finished the chart, choose three of those inventions and describe why you believe they were so important.

CULTURE OR CIVILIZATION		
1.	2.	3.
INVENTIONS OR ADVANCES		

2. After the terrorist attacks of 9/11 in the United States, many subjects were discussed and argued, including what it means to be a hero. The police officers and firefighters who assisted people after the attacks in New York were often referred to as heroes, while some people countered that they were just doing their jobs. To the ancient Celts, a hero like Cuchulainn had great strength and was able to overpower his enemies and protect his people. There was something superhuman about Cuchulainn, just as there was about Hercules. Superhuman abilities seem to be very popular in the tales and fantasies of many cultures. Just look at how popular comic book heroes like Spiderman and Superman are. Have you ever wished you could possess super powers? What would those powers be? What would you use them for?

3. Love was a very popular theme in ancient myths, just as it is today. Researchers argue that the stories of King Arthur are tied to the ancient Celts, including the love story between the great hero Lancelot and Guinevere, the wife of King Arthur. The stories of knights of medieval Europe often describe them not only with the Celtic qualities of courage and strength found in Cuchulainn, but with the passion of Cuchulainn as well. Do you think you could write such a tale of love and romance? Give it a try. Create your characters, thinking not only of how they look, but also their personalities and strengths and weaknesses. How will they interact? How will they fall in love? And what adventures would they face together?

POLITICAL SCIENCE

Political Science, as the name suggests, is the science or study of politics—the study of political theory, public law, and public administration. However, "politics" may not mean exactly what you think it does. Politics is not only what happens in state or national capitols. It is not exclusively the domain of politicians and presidents and members of parliament. In fact, you could argue that politics derives from any situation in which groups of people must live and interact with one another on a day-to-day basis, each with his or her own skills and needs and fears and desires. Politics, in other words, is how we maintain order in such a potentially chaotic and disordered community of striving and grasping and giving individuals.

Discuss with your peers each of the following types of government. What form does such a government take? How many people are involved in such a government? How do they gain power? What limits are there to their authority? What role do the people have in creating or participating in these governments? As you talk about these issues, write out a description of each type of government.

1. anarchy _____
   _____
   _____

2. aristocracy _____
   _____
   _____

3. autocracy _____
   _____
   _____

4. democracy _____
   _____
   _____

5. dictatorship _____
   _____
   _____

6. military junta _____
   _____
   _____

7. monarchy _____
   _____
   _____

8. theocracy _____
   _____
   _____

POLITICAL SCIENCE

A. *Here are our target vocabulary for Reading 1 in this unit:*

apparently	exercise	perspective	role
authority	function	prohibit	significant
concept	institution	reform	tension

B. *Look at the following vocabulary words in context. Can you find synonyms in the text to help you understand the meaning of the highlighted words? Circle the synonyms you find.*

1. This is not to say that ancient Athenian democracy was the same **institution**—or even a similar organization, really—as our modern American democracy. *(lines 4–6)*

2. Before we go on to analyze the **concept** of democracy in the United States—the notion of a government by the people—it might be worthwhile to pause at this time and consider the actual Greek origins of democracy. *(lines 6–8)*

3. The state was everything, and the **function** of the people was to serve the state. This purpose was their only reason for existing—at least from the state's **perspective**, a viewpoint that the people naturally could not share. *(lines 19–21)*

4. During the proceeding Archaic Era of Greece, power in many Greek city-states was held by aristocratic families whose **authority** stemmed from two sources. *(lines 22–24)*

5. The Athenians suffered from social **tensions**—the same strains that led the masses of other cities to call for revolution. *(lines 33–34)*

6. The Council of Areopagus chose a fellow aristocrat named Solon to function as archon, the highest official of the state, with the power to **reform** or modify the legal system. *(lines 38–40)*

7. Having achieved his reforms, Solon took a **significant** step—a very important step indeed—he left Athens in order to avoid pressure for further reform as well as to avoid popular calls for him to take up a position as tyrant. *(lines 68–71)*

8. And to make sure there was no corruption, Pericles instituted the position of government spies, whose **role** was to watch over the officials and report any unethical activity to Pericles himself. *(lines 116–18)*

C. *You can improve your vocabulary by going beyond simply learning words and their meanings. Instead, when you learn a new verb, for example, pay attention to the objects that usually accompany that verb. In each of the following sentences, underline the verb "exercise" and circle the object of the verb.*

1. Considering how far in debt you are, I think you should exercise a little caution before you go out and buy an expensive brand new car.

2. The police were very persistent, but Samson chose to exercise his rights by refusing to answer any more questions until his lawyer arrived to advise him on the matter.

3. Sure, Sara is exercising more often these days, but I have seen her go straight from the gym to the nearest fast food restaurant. She really should exercise some restraint when it comes to her diet.

4. I'm telling you—Matthew is not a good friend to you. He exercises too much influence over you—over your behavior, your beliefs, and your thoughts. You need to think for yourself.

5. You may not want to hear it, but I am going to exercise my freedom of speech and tell you exactly what I think about your new alternative lifestyle.

D. *Now choose three of the objects above and write your own sentences with the verb "exercise" and those objects.*

1. _____
   _____

2. _____
   _____

3. _____
   _____

E. *Circle the vocabulary word that best completes each of the following sentences.*

1. Patricia is quite happy that she chose to attend classes here. She said that this is the best *concept / function / institution* of learning she has ever attended.

2. The idea behind your proposal is a good one, but it simply won't make a good law as it is now. You should *exercise / prohibit / reform* your proposal before you submit it.

3. There must be limits to the *authority / perspective / role* that a president exercises. Otherwise, the rights of the people will suffer under his power.

4. The news has focused a lot of attention on the *authority / function / tension* between the President and Congress lately. Do you think that Congress might try to impeach the President?

5. What made Governor Stevens so effective was that he brought a completely new *concept / perspective / reform* to his role as governor, seeing things in a whole new way.

6. If the government votes to *exercise / prohibit / reform* guns in our schools, I will feel much safer.

POLITICAL SCIENCE

Active reading can help you better understand a college text. Begin by discussing the questions below. Then carefully read the following essay, taking notes on the main points and important details, characters, and events that you find in the text. Also select the best meaning for words highlighted in the right-hand column.

PREREADING DISCUSSION

Ancient Greece is described in western education as a classical civilization—a culture of diverse and significant innovations. What do you know about ancient Greece? Can you describe any inventions or innovations that began in Greece? What other great civilizations are you familiar with? What innovations stemmed from those cultures?

(1)   It is appropriate that the term "politics" derives from an ancient Greek word—appropriate insofar as the legacy of government and social order embraced by many nations today was first theorized and put into practice in ancient Athens. This is not to say that ancient Athenian democracy was the same

5   institution—or even a similar organization, really—as our modern American democracy. Before we go on to analyze the concept of democracy in the United States—the notion of a government by the people—it might be worthwhile to pause at this time and consider the actual Greek origins of democracy. It would not be an exaggeration, I think, to say that an ancient Athenian would not only

10   disapprove of our democratic system, but would hardly consider it to be democratic at all.

> **line 1: term**
>
> *a.*   word
> *b.*   period
> *c.*   tenure
>
> **Another example:**
> *Do you know the term for "government" in Spanish?*

(2)   To begin with, we should acknowledge that two and a half millennia ago there was no nation-state of Greece. Rather, in the regions of what today is modern Greece, there were a number of city-states, including Athens, which were

15   ruled by monarchs—kings who exercised absolute power. There were no written laws; the king's word was law, as it was in Egypt and throughout the ancient world until Babylonian rulers such as Ur-Nammu and Hammurabi had laws codified for all to obey. Nor was there any popular participation in government. The state was everything, and the function of the people was to serve the state.

20   This purpose was their only reason for existing—at least from the state's perspective, a viewpoint that the people naturally could not share.

(3)   During the proceeding Archaic Era of Greece, power in many Greek city-states was held by aristocratic families whose authority stemmed from two sources: 1) ownership of arable land with the wealth this brought one, and 2)

25   military leadership, also a result of wealth in a land in which ownership of metal weapons and horses was costly. The form this aristocratic government took in Athens was the Council of Areopagus, a council of representatives of the 100 wealthiest landowning families. Each year these men would choose from among their own ranks an *archon*. The *archon*, who filled the role of the highest

30   authority of the land, exercised a number of the functions previously exercised by the Greek monarchs. However, his powers were strictly limited by the Council and by their rigidly observed single year terms.

The Law Code of Hammurabi (c.1772 BC)

(4)   The Athenians suffered from social tensions—the same strains that led the masses of other cities to call for revolution. More and more Athenians were

35   becoming enslaved by the wealthy Athenians to whom they were indebted. Meanwhile, economic, legislative, and political monopolies were held by certain aristocratic families of Athens. In 594 BC, after continued pressure from below and from within their own class, the Council of Areopagus chose a fellow

40   aristocrat named Solon to function as *archon*, the highest official of the state, with the power to reform or modify the legal system. The popular image of Solon was that of a poet, philosopher, and statesman, but most importantly an aristocrat who blamed his own class for the sufferings of the people. In fact, he was apparently quite public in his denunciation of the upper class to which he belonged, accusing them of growing rich through "unrighteous deeds."

45   (5)   Considering his populist approach to social change, it is not at all surprising that Solon's most popular reforms freed the masses from bondage to the aristocrats. This *seisachtheia* or "shaking off of burdens," Solon's first important action as *archon*, declared a number of revolutionary reforms in Athens. While debts were not cancelled, some relief of debts was offered by the

50   state. The many Athenians who had been forced into servitude as involuntary share-croppers or sold into slavery because of their indebtedness were restored to freedom. Athenians sold abroad as slaves were brought back home. And a new law prohibited anyone from mortgaging the persons of free men or women as security for their debts.

55   (6)   These were stunning reforms, but Solon did not stop there. Records for Solon's complete tenure in office are sketchy, but he apparently initiated government reforms that would finally open up government offices to more people, even among the poor. At the top of the government hierarchy remained the aristocratic Council

60   of Areopagus, but now new government offices were created for the middle class as well. They were now eligible for the first time for minor offices and for the Council of 400, a group of upper middle class men who advised the aristocrats. Meanwhile, the poor could serve on the People's Assembly, which could influence

65   the selection of archons. Finally, any laws enacted by the new government had to be written down.

Atop the Acropolis of ancient Athens

(7)   Having achieved his reforms, Solon took a significant step—a very important step indeed—he left Athens in order to avoid pressure for further reform as well as to avoid popular calls for him to take up a position as tyrant.

70   Others were not quite as noble as Solon, and from 545-510 BC Athens was ruled by increasingly dictatorial tyrants. Then in the year 510, following rising tension, another reforming aristocrat took power. His name was Kleisthenes, and once in power, he set about redefining the concept of democracy and strengthening the democratic institutions begun by Solon.

75   (8)   Kleisthenes reformed the electoral system, which had previously allowed people to vote according to their clans. This old system regularly led to people voting for the traditional leaders of their own clans, which encouraged greater factionalism in government. The new electoral system divided the population according to the district they inhabited, rather than the clan they belonged to.

80   Thus, no elected official could count on the unanimous backing of his clan. Rather he had a much larger and more diverse constituency to please. As a further check on any particular individual gaining too much power, Kleisthenes instituted the process of ostracism. With ostracism, once a year the population had the authority to expel one unwanted individual from Athens for ten years.

85   (9)   Moreover, Kleisthenes introduced a democratic constitution that gave all 45,000 male citizens the right to attend the Assembly and vote on all major

decisions and appointments. In theory, all public policy was determined by vote of the Assembly, and all government officials were responsible to the Assembly alone. No one could challenge or alter its decision, although in practice the
90   aristocratic Council of Areopagus continued to wield a great deal of political influence. Through the Assembly, any adult male citizen could propose legislation, and whenever a proposal was to be voted on, all 45,000 citizens had the right to step forward and cast their votes directly, rather than waiting for an elected representative to vote on their behalf. Public debate could not be
95   prohibited. This meant that people could publically criticize and speak of removing their leaders from power without fear of retaliation.

(10)   The democratic institutions that had been evolving over the last century were put into their final form by Pericles (r.462-429 BC). Thanks to Pericles and the people of Athens, this new democracy proved durable enough to endure for
100   140 years, until the conquest of Greece by the Romans. Ultimate power was held by the citizens through the Assembly, which functioned as the legislative and to some extent as the executive branch of government. All decisions were made by a simple majority vote. Service in the Assembly was open to all adult male citizens. However, other obligations and the long journey into town prohibited
105   many rural citizens from attending. Pericles therefore commanded that salaries be provided for all public officials and members of the armed forces, which enabled the poorer class of citizens to participate in government as well.

*Statue of Pericles
in Paris, France*

(11)   Most public officials were selected by lot, so as to ensure that no official could buy his way into office. Election by lot meant that at any one time, the
110   vast majority of officials serving the city of Athens were not professional politicians or bureaucrats, but interested citizens, devoting one or two years of their life to the proper maintenance and functioning of their city. Since all public officials were limited to short terms of office, most wealthy or greedy individuals had no interest in serving anyway—they could not stay in office long enough to
115   benefit from their corrupt actions. And to make sure there was no corruption, Pericles instituted the position of government spies, whose role was to watch over the officials and report any unethical activity to Pericles himself.

(12)   Finally, Pericles expanded the popular law courts. The first thing a modern reader notices concerning these popular courts was the absence of judges
120   and lawyers. The decision of the court was made by a jury of citizens—chosen by lots, of course. The typical size of a jury was 501, although juries could be as small as 51 and as large as 1,501 depending on how significant the case was. At the end of the hearing, the jury would make its decision using secret ballots. A simple majority decided the case. No lawyers were involved in Athenian court
125   cases; they were argued instead by the private citizens involved, although some plaintiffs and defendants hired professional speech writers to assist them.

line 122: case
a.   box
b.   occurrence
c.   trial
Another example:
Yesterday Judge Carden dismissed the case against the government.

(13)   No matter the case, time was strictly limited; no case was allowed to last
more than one day. With a decision of guilt or innocence, a further decision concerning proper penalties might be required. Most laws did not specify
130   penalties, and therefore the plaintiff and defendant generally suggested their own penalties. The jury would take these suggestions into consideration when deciding what they felt to be an appropriate penalty. To discourage frivolous cases, a further fine would be applied to any plaintiff who failed to win a certain percentage of the jury to his side.[10]

POLITICAL SCIENCE

A. *Which of the following statements best expresses the main point that the writer of "Evolution of Democracy" is trying to make?*

1. While many nations today embrace a form of democracy, a different type of democratic government evolved long ago in ancient Athens.

2. The ancient Greeks demonstrated their advanced civilization in many ways, including in their invention of the democratic form of government.

3. While many cultures strive for democracy in the world today, they owe their gratitude to the founders of democratic principles in ancient Athens.

B. *Read the following statements. Do they agree with the information in the essay? Circle T (true) or F (false) for each statement.*

1. T   F   Democracy was invented over 2,000 years ago in the nation-state of Greece.
2. T   F   The *archon* was the highest official of the ancient Athenian government.
3. T   F   During the time of Kleisthenes there were 45,000 men and women in Athens.
4. T   F   Pericles of Athens was born in the year 462 BC.
5. T   F   The Council of Areopagus were representatives of the 100 richest families.
6. T   F   Under Pericles, the ultimate ruling power was held by the citizens of Athens.
7. T   F   Ostracism allowed Athenians to expel someone from Athens for life.

C. *Skim through the essay once again and write the name of the man who invented each of the following elements of the Athenian system of democracy: Solon, Kleisthenes, or Pericles.*

1. _____ Court cases were limited to no more than one day in length.
2. _____ Spies were used to ensure that government officials were not corrupt.
3. _____ Emancipated people who had been sold into slavery because of debts.
4. _____ Freedom of speech was protected for the first time.
5. _____ The People's Assembly was created to allow even the poorest citizens a role in the government.
6. _____ A new electoral system prohibited people from simply voting for their own family members for government office.
7. _____ Juries were composed of citizens selected at random by lot.
8. _____ All laws enacted by the government had to be written down.
9. _____ The aristocrats remained at the top of the government.
10. _____ All public policy was determined by the vote of the Assembly.

D. Pronouns such as HE, SHE, IT, and THEY are often used in texts to avoid repeating names and concepts that should be understood without directly naming them. However, the complexity of an academic text can make it quite challenging to follow the text if you do not know who or what the pronouns refer to. Take your time with pronouns. Do not just skip over them. Make sure you know what they mean in a text. Look at the following sentences from the reading "Evolution of Democracy." In the space provided, write WHO or WHAT the underlined pronoun refers to. Keep in mind that the pronoun "it" sometimes does not refer to anything at all. This so-called "dummy IT" is used to provide a SUBJECT for a sentence that has no subject. For example, in the sentence "It is cold outside," the subject "It" does not refer to anything. If the pronoun below is a "dummy IT," then write "no reference."

1. _____ <u>It</u> is appropriate that the term "politics" derives from an ancient Greek word. *(lines 1–2)*

2. _____ <u>It</u> might be worthwhile to pause at this time and consider the actual Greek origins of democracy. *(lines 7–8)*

3. _____ The king's word was law, as <u>it</u> was in Egypt and throughout the ancient world until Babylonian rulers such as Ur-Nammu and Hammurabi had laws codified for all to obey. *(lines 16–18)*

4. _____ However, <u>his</u> powers were strictly limited by the Council and by their rigidly observed single year terms. *(lines 31–32)*

5. _____ In 594 BC, after continued pressure from below and from within <u>their</u> own class, the Council of Areopagus chose a fellow aristocrat named Solon to function as *archon*. *(lines 37–39)*

6. _____ <u>It</u> is not at all surprising that Solon's most popular reforms freed the masses from bondage to the aristocrats. *(lines 45–47)*

7. _____ And a new law prohibited anyone from mortgaging the persons of free men or women as security for <u>their</u> debts. *(lines 52–54)*

8. _____ <u>They</u> were now eligible for the first time for minor offices and for the Council of 400. *(lines 61–62)*

9. _____ Then in the year 510, following rising tension, another reforming aristocrat took power. <u>His</u> name was Kleisthenes. *(lines 71–72)*

10. _____ Thus, no elected official could count on the unanimous backing of his clan. Rather <u>he</u> had a much larger and more diverse constituency to please. *(lines 80–81)*

11. _____ All public policy was determined by vote of the Assembly, and all government officials were responsible to the Assembly alone. No one could challenge or alter <u>its</u> decision. *(lines 87–89)*

12. _____ The democratic institutions that had been evolving over the last century were put into <u>their</u> final form by Pericles (r.462–429 BC). *(lines 97–98)*

13. _____ No lawyers were involved in Athenian court cases; <u>they</u> were argued instead by the private citizens involved. *(lines 124–25)*

POLITICAL SCIENCE

A. THE FORM AND FUNCTION OF THE PASSIVE VOICE

The **passive** form of a verb is not a tense. It is often referred to as a *"voice"*—the passive voice, which can be used with all of the same verb tenses in which the active voice can be expressed. When using the passive voice, the object of the sentence is moved to the beginning of the sentence and becomes the subject.

> **ACTIVE**: Thomas Jefferson wrote the <u>Declaration of Independence</u>. →
>   **object**

> **PASSIVE**: The <u>Declaration of Independence</u> was written by Thomas Jefferson.
>   **subject**

Notice the use of the preposition **"by"** before the actor of a passive sentence—*"by Thomas Jefferson"*. The active and passive sentences in this example describe the same **actor** (Thomas Jefferson), the same **action** (writing), and the same **object** (the Declaration of Independence). However, by using the passive voice, the speaker or writer is trying to focus your attention on the **object** of a sentence, rather than on the **actor**. This may be for several reasons:

    a.   the object is more important than the actor

> ### The largest pyramid in the ancient world was built by the Egyptians.
> *[The focus is on this being "the largest pyramid."]*

    b.   the actor is so obvious that it does not need to be mentioned

> ### Your letter was delivered yesterday at 5:00 p.m.
> *[It is obvious that your letter was delivered by the postman.]*

    c.   we do not know who or what the actor is

> ### These cave paintings were made about 25,000 years ago.
> *[We don't know the identity of the people who made these paintings.]*

Of the three examples above, only sentence **(a)** tells you the **actor** of the sentence—*"the Egyptians."* In sentences **(b)** and **(c)** no actor is given. This is quite common with passive sentences. If the actor is **obvious** [example **(b)**] or **unknown** [example **(c)**], then no actor is necessary. Look at the following sentences. There is an actor in each sentence and an object that is acted on (which becomes the subject in a passive sentence). If the actor is **unnecessary** in these sentences, cross it out. For example:

> ### Tammy was operated on last week ~~by a doctor~~.

1.   My favorite novel ever was written by Charles Dickens.

2.   The suspected killer of Martin Smith was finally captured last night by the police.

3.   Our famous lemon and lentil soup is prepared fresh every day by our cook.

4.   The first form of democracy in the western world was invented in Athens by Solon.

5.   The Great Wall of China was built over a period of two millennia by many workers.

6.   Barack Obama was elected as the forty fourth president of the United States by the voters.

7.   The division of the US government into the executive, legislative, and judicial branches was established by the Constitution.

8.   Unlike Jamestown, Virginia, the city of New York was settled by the Dutch.

B. *In each of the following passive sentences from the essay "Evolution of Democracy," circle the passive verb. Then underline and number (1) the __object__ of the verb (which has become the subject of the passive sentence), and (2) the __actor__ of the verb if the actor is included in the sentence. For example:*

The ⁽¹⁾<u>People's Assembly</u> (was created) by ⁽²⁾<u>Solon.</u>

1. The legacy of government and social order embraced by many nations today was first theorized and put into practice in ancient Athens. *(lines 2–4)*

2. During the proceeding Archaic Era of Greece, power in many Greek city-states was held by aristocratic families. *(lines 22–23)*

3. His powers were strictly limited by the Council and by their rigidly observed single year terms. *(lines 31–32)*

4. Meanwhile, economic, legislative, and political monopolies were held by certain aristocratic families of Athens. *(lines 36–37)*

5. While debts were not cancelled, some relief of debts was offered by the state. *(lines 49–50)*

6. New government offices were created for the middle class as well. *(lines 60–61)*

7. In theory, all public policy was determined by vote of the Assembly. *(lines 87–88)*

8. Public debate could not be prohibited. *(lines 94–95)*

9. Ultimate power was held by the citizens through the Assembly. *(lines 100–01)*

10. All decisions were made by a simple majority vote. *(lines 102–03)*

C. *Choose from the verbs below to complete the following sentences. Write the verbs in the passive voice.*

achieve	compose	devote	expose	indicate	reform
approach	declare	ensure	illustrate	prohibit	seize

1. The road that we need to take to get to the capitol _____ on the map by a dark blue line.

2. The sale of alcohol _____ by the US government in 1919.

3. Charles Dickens' beloved story of *A Christmas Carol* _____ by an artist and actor named John Leech, who drew some very famous cartoons.

4. Independence for the United States _____ in 1776 by the man who would become the nation's third president—Thomas Jefferson.

5. The most famous explanation of communist principles—the *Communist Manifesto*— _____ in 1848 by Karl Marx and Friedrich Engels.

6. The revolting conditions within the US meat packing industry, including the presence of rats packed with the meat, _____ by Upton Sinclair in 1906.

7. The goals of our committee _____ last month with the enactment of the new law on equal rights for all workers.

8. Our home _____ by the bank when we couldn't pay the mortgage.

POLITICAL SCIENCE

Choose from the following options for your journal writing assignment:

1. We began this chapter by considering different types of government and looked more in depth at the origin of democracy. Would democracy be your government of choice? Do you think democracy is the best government for all people? In the chart below, write a few key notes to compare and contrast the pros and cons of democracy along with two other types of government.

democracy		
pros		
cons		

Now write out your analysis of these three types of government in essay form.

2. The aristocracy of ancient Athens strictly controlled the process of enacting new laws. However, the creators of democracy believed that the people themselves should be involved—even directly involved—in legislating. That is, the people should be lawmakers. Imagine that you are a legislator. What kind of laws would you choose to enact? Describe your ideal laws. Why are they important to you? What country do you believe needs to have such laws? Who would benefit from them?

3. Not all laws have a positive affect over the people, do they? On 16 January 1919, the United States ratified the Eighteenth Amendment to the Constitution, which prohibited the "manufacture, sale, or transportation of intoxicating liquors within, the importation thereof into, or the exportation thereof from the United States..." With the Eighteenth Amendment, it became a crime in the United States to make, sell, or transport alcohol. However, on 5 December 1933, the government passed the Twenty-first Amendment, which repealed the Eighteenth Amendment. Alcohol was again legal in the US. What laws have you encountered in the US or in any other country that you believe should be repealed? What was wrong with those laws? Why do you think they were enacted in the first place?

POLITICAL SCIENCE   VOCABULARY 4.2

A. *Here are our target vocabulary for our next reading on "Early American Democracy." Draw a line to match each vocabulary word to the most appropriate definition.*

1.	administration	**a.**	A contract that establishes rights and responsibilities.
2.	category	**b.**	A managing or governing authority.
3.	charter	**c.**	Basically or principally true.
4.	colonist	**d.**	Involvement in an activity or group.
5.	discipline	**e.**	A group or class into which things are divided.
6.	essentially	**f.**	Control over organization and behavior.
7.	establish	**g.**	Limited or prohibited in some way.
8.	participation	**h.**	Someone who settles away from the mother country.
9.	principle	**i.**	To fight or work hard to achieve a goal.
10.	restricted	**j.**	To found or create a colony or institution.
11.	struggle	**k.**	Patience or understanding with differences.
12.	toleration	**l.**	Central belief or rule that governs conduct.

B. *Below are different forms of two of our vocabulary words: "essentially" and "restricted." Write the letters of the words in each list that best complete the sentences.*

1. In this class, we will not study all aspects of Psychology. We will only learn the _____ .

2. The _____ difference between these two directors concerns how they show violence in their movies.

3. You do not need to write about your high school education on this application. That is _____ information.

   a. essence
   b. essential
   c. essentials
   d. essentially
   e. nonessential

4. The Governor is trying to _____ access to assault weapons in the state.

5. The director has given me _____ access to the museum. I can basically see everything they have got here!

6. As a foreign student, Tamara did not know that there were _____ on where she was allowed to work. I'm afraid she applied for the wrong job.

   f. restrict
   g. restricted
   h. restrictive
   i. restrictions
   j. unrestricted

C. When you learn new vocabulary, take the time to consider the different forms of those words. How would we write the different parts of speech for the following vocabulary words? Use a dictionary to help you complete the chart below. Some forms of the words do not exist or are unnecessary to complete the chart.

	VERB	*NOUN*	*ADJECTIVE*	*ADVERB*
1.		administration		
2.		category		
3.		colonist		
4.		discipline		
5.				essentially
6.	establish			
7.		participation		
8.			restricted	
9.		toleration		

D. Look again at the nine groups of words in Part C. Choose two words each from four of those groups and write sentences with them. For example:

a. My father **administers** a company that sells computer software.

b. Sometimes he has to make difficult **administrative** decisions about his company.

1. a. _____

   _____

   b. _____

   _____

2. a. _____

   _____

   b. _____

   _____

3. a. _____

   _____

   b. _____

   _____

4. a. _____

   _____

   b. _____

   _____

POLITICAL SCIENCE

Discuss the questions below with your peers. Then carefully read the following essay on "Early American Democracy," taking notes on the main points and important details, figures, and events that you find in the text. Also select the best meaning for words highlighted in the right-hand column.

PREREADING DISCUSSION

1. What is democracy like in the United States today? How different does it seem to you from the form of democracy that we have read about in ancient Athens?
2. What do you know about the British colonies of North America before the United States declared its independence from Britain? What kind of freedoms did the colonists enjoy?
3. Do you know the story of Pocahontas and John Smith? What happened to them?

(1)   The democratic institutions of the United States have long been upheld as exemplary in the development of democracy in the modern world. While American democracy is quite distinct from the democratic institutions established in ancient Athens, both forms of democracy have embraced similar principles: a
5   just and written legal code, freedom and equality for all citizens, and the participation of the people in governing themselves. Likewise, both Athenian and American democracy were restricted by essentially undemocratic beliefs and practices. Just as the ancient Athenians defined "citizen" in a limited way—based on categories of race, ethnicity, wealth, and gender—so too did United
10 States Americans.

(2)   Much has been written about the democratic character of the British colonies in North America with their seeds of democracy, such as town hall meetings. In these public meetings, people could express their opinions and negotiate decisions about public matters. However, if you could look into the
15 very first successful English colony in the Americas—Jamestown—you would see nothing like a democratic administration. On the contrary, the first British colonists in the New World lived under what might best be described as a military dictatorship. This dictatorship was ruled for a short time by a man who has become synonymous in American cinema with kindness towards Native
20 Americans—Captain John Smith (c.1580–1631).

(3)   The Jamestown of John Smith was established by a charter granted by the English King James I (r.1603–1625). Thanks to stories of wealth and vast tracts of land in the New World—stories brought back to the Old World by Christopher Columbus and his successors—the race was on among European
25 crowns to lay claim to the riches of a colonial empire. On 10 April 1606, King James therefore granted charters to two separate companies to settle in the Americas. The first of these British colonies was established in what is today Maine, but it disintegrated when the local Indians fought back against the aggressive British colonists and when the harsh winters proved too much for the
30 Europeans to endure.

(4)   Jamestown itself nearly failed as well. The company that held the charter for Jamestown—the Virginia Company of London—sent 105 colonists to the New World in 1607 aboard ships like the Discovery. They established Jamestown near Chesapeake Bay in what is today the state of Virginia.
35 However, many of these colonists were little more than treasure seekers, hoping to find gold and get rich quickly. They had little interest in building homes or

A statue of Captain John Smith on Jamestown Island

cultivating crops, and consequently when winter came, many starved to death. When a ship arrived in January 1608 to bring them food and aid, they found only 38 people left alive.

40   (5)   In September of that year, the Virginia Company decided to take a tougher stand on ensuring the colony's survival—they placed the administration of the colony under Captain John Smith. Smith was a military man who had seen action fighting against the Turks and the Spanish. He quickly assessed that the colony needed discipline and required order. He commanded them to construct

45   homes and cultivate lands while he sought to improve relations with the Native American Powhatan Confederacy, which had been suspicious of and sometimes hostile to the colony. The story of Pocahontas—daughter of Powhatan, chief of the confederacy—saving Smith's life is likely untrue. Nor is it likely that there was ever any romantic relationship between Smith and Pocahontas. Nonetheless,

50   Smith's struggle did succeed in reviving the failing colony, which firmly established an English foothold in the Americas, although not a democratic one.

    (6)   So when did democracy emerge in the Americas? It has long been suggested that colonists from England made the dangerous Atlantic voyage to the New World to own property and freely exercise their religions. This has been

55   acknowledged as a seed at least of democracy in the Americas. Once again, there is some exaggeration in this. Surely the most famous religious movement to arrive in the northern British colonies was the Puritan movement represented by the Pilgrims who voyaged to Plymouth, Massachusetts in a ship called the Mayflower. The Puritans were a militant and reformist church. They were

60   dissatisfied with how slowly the Church of England was reforming the faith and cleansing it of Catholic traditions. The Church of England was just not pure enough for the Puritans.

    (7)   Thus, the Pilgrims left Europe and traveled to the Americas. However, while it is true that the Puritans were eager to leave a nation hostile to their

65   puritanical form of Christianity and to worship freely in accordance with their beliefs, this does not mean that they welcomed democratic or religious freedoms. On the contrary, Puritans established a form of theocracy in the colony with the Bible as the foundation of law. The leaders strictly ruled the settlers according to their own fundamentalist Christian principles and displayed no toleration for any

70   other religion, especially a Native American one. Acceptance in the colony of Plymouth was typically tied to faith, and attendance in church was mandatory for all members of the faith. Moral discipline was considered critical in the upbringing of children. At the age of eight, many children were handed over to foster families out of fear that their own parents might spoil them rather than

75   raise the children with the discipline required by the Puritan faith.

    (8)   The United States has long struggled to provide equality for all people, a struggle that continues today. Insofar as people associate equality with democracy, then once again we would find little to praise in the early colonies that would become the United States of America. The treatment of Native Americans

80   was atrocious. At best they were tolerated as naïve and primitive creatures; at worst, they were abused, enslaved, and slaughtered. Africans fared no better, of course. By the end of the nineteenth century, some 12 million Africans had been transported against their will to the Americas to serve Europeans and their descendants as slaves. Just before the abolition of slavery in the United States,

85   the African slave population in the US numbered around four million.

---

line 54: exercise

a. work out
b. use
c. practice

Another example:
After immigrating to the US, many people still exercise their native culture.

The Mayflower II at Plymouth, Massachusetts

line 74: spoil

a. indulge
b. ruin
c. decay

Another example:
From the way that Matt behaves, it is obvious that he was spoiled as a child.

(9)   However, a more limited form of slavery thrived for a time in the colonies and in the US in the form of indentured servitude. Indentured servants were migrants to the New World who could not afford to pay for their passage and so instead signed a contract with a wealthier individual—a patron or master.
90   The master paid for the servant to cross the water, and once here, the servant essentially belonged to the master for a period typically of 4–7 years. At the end of that contract, the servant could go free … in theory. However, some 40 percent of these servants died during their servitude, often from the harsh treatment they endured. Moreover, a servant who became pregnant during her
95   servitude could be punished by having more years added to her contract.

(10)   Apart from the obvious inequalities associated with slavery and indentured servitude, the Puritan ethic that dominated the New England colonies defined women in a clearly subordinate position to their fathers and husbands. By obeying her husband, a good woman set for her children an example of moral
100   behavior and obedience. Yet in contrast to a woman in England, an American wife enjoyed legal protection from an abusive husband and could seek to dissolve the marriage if her husband was severely negligent, cruel, or adulterous. At least that is what the law allowed her to do. In practice, few divorces were granted. Between 1639–1692, the courts of Massachusetts granted only 27 divorces.

105   (11)   In contrast to the Puritans of Massachusetts, the Protestants of Rhode Island lived under a considerable degree of toleration for diverse cultures and faiths. And this was thanks to one man in particular—Roger Williams. Williams (c.1603–1683) was a Protestant theologian and a keen member of the Puritan movement. He was convinced that the Church of England could never be
110   cleansed and must therefore be abandoned. However, he insisted on the principle of religious freedom for all people—Puritans and non-Puritans alike. Every man and woman, he argued, must be allowed to worship according to their own convictions, and the church must forever be kept separate from the government. This meant that Williams was one of the first to promote the secular democratic
115   principle—upheld by the Bill of Rights—of the separation of church and state.

line 106: degree
a. temperature
b. amount
c. diploma
Another example:
We need a greater degree of discipline to keep our workers productive.

(12)   Williams' criticism of the royal charters—the very charters that granted land to the Jamestown and Plymouth colonists—caused concern among his fellow Puritans. They were especially displeased when Williams argued that the Puritans had taken land away from the Native Americans without compensating
120   the Indians for the land. Permission from the British government was not enough; colonists should pay Indians for the lands that the colonists inhabit. The authorities of Massachusetts demanded an explanation from Williams and his oath of allegiance to the royal governor. Williams refused. In 1635, Williams was convicted of heresy by the General Court and ordered to leave the colony.

125   (13)   The next year, Williams and his small band of followers arrived in Rhode Island. There he acquired permission from Canonicus and Miantonomi, representatives of the Narragansett natives—not from the British King Charles I—to settle on an area of land that he named Providence. The colony of Providence followed the principle of religious freedom for all and the separation
130   of church and state. The administration of Providence was only allowed to make decisions on civil matters, not religious ones. Government decisions depended on a majority vote by the heads of the households of the town. In 1640, 39 citizens of Providence once more confirmed their conviction "still to hold forth liberty of conscience."

line 128: name
a. accuse
b. term
c. choose
Another example:
I wonder why the settlers named this town Bountiful when it is so empty.

POLITICAL SCIENCE

A. Which of the following statements best expresses the main point that the writer of "Early American Democracy" is trying to make?

1. Early Americans had much in common with the ancient Greeks, including their aspirations for a democratic society.

2. Men like John Smith and Roger Williams ensured that American citizens would enjoy the freedoms protected by a democratic state.

3. While the United States has struggled to establish democratic freedoms for all, the early colonial administrations in the Americas were far from democratic.

B. Quickly scan through the essay and find two names for each of the following categories.

1. English colonies   **a.** _____   **b.** _____

2. US states   **a.** _____   **b.** _____

3. Colonial leaders   **a.** _____   **b.** _____

4. Religious groups   **a.** _____   **b.** _____

5. Indian tribes   **a.** _____   **b.** _____

6. Native Americans   **a.** _____   **b.** _____

7. Colonial ships   **a.** _____   **b.** _____

8. British kings   **a.** _____   **b.** _____

C. Read the following statements. Do they agree with the information in the essay? Circle T (true) or F (false) for each statement.

1.	T	F	Unlike citizenship in Athens, citizenship in the early US was open to all people.
2.	T	F	Town hall meetings were an early form of democracy in America.
3.	T	F	The kings of Europe raced to claim land in the Americas because it was such a beautiful place to settle.
4.	T	F	King James granted charters for settlements in Maine and Virginia.
5.	T	F	The Puritans were fundamentalist Christians opposed to the Catholic Church.
6.	T	F	Puritan children sometimes lived in foster homes to learn more discipline.
7.	T	F	Like most slaves from Africa, indentured servants could never be freed.
8.	T	F	Unlike back in England, divorce in Massachusetts was very common.
9.	T	F	Roger Williams believed the government should support Puritanism.
10.	T	F	The colony of Providence was established on land purchased from Indians.

D. *As you know, many words in English have more than one meaning. A simple word such as "hold" has several dozen different meanings depending on the context in which the word is used. For example, look at the meaning of "hold" in the following sentences:*

a.	*I saw a man outside <u>holding</u> a gun.*	→	*to have in one's hand*
b.	*We <u>hold</u> you responsible for this mistake.*	→	*to maintain or claim*
c.	*She <u>holds</u> with an uncommon religious belief.*	→	*to follow or adhere to*

Circle the letter of the meaning that is closest to the underlined word in the following sentences.

1. The democratic institutions of the United States have long been <u>upheld</u> as exemplary in the development of democracy in the modern world. *(lines 1–2)*
   - **a.** lifted up
   - **b.** defended
   - **c.** stolen

2. …both forms of democracy have <u>embraced</u> similar principles: a just and written legal code, freedom and equality for all citizens, and the participation of the people in governing themselves. *(lines 4–6)*
   - **a.** willingly accepted
   - **b.** held close
   - **c.** seized

3. Much has been written about the democratic <u>character</u> of the British colonies in North America with their seeds of democracy, such as town hall meetings. *(lines 11–13)*
   - **a.** nature
   - **b.** actor
   - **c.** personality

4. On 10 April 1606, King James therefore granted charters to two separate companies to <u>settle</u> in the Americas. *(lines 25–27)*
   - **a.** agree on
   - **b.** pay off
   - **c.** colonize

5. They established Jamestown near Chesapeake Bay in what is today the <u>state</u> of Virginia. *(lines 33–34)*
   - **a.** condition
   - **b.** status
   - **c.** territory

6. In September of that year, the Virginia Company decided to take a tougher <u>stand</u> on ensuring the colony's survival. *(lines 40–41)*
   - **a.** policy
   - **b.** station
   - **c.** platform

7. The story of Pocahontas—daughter of Powhatan, <u>chief</u> of the confederacy—saving Smith's life is likely untrue. *(lines 47–48)*
   - **a.** highest
   - **b.** principal
   - **c.** leader

8. Surely the most famous religious <u>movement</u> to arrive in the northern British colonies was the Puritan movement represented by the Pilgrims who voyaged to Plymouth, Massachusetts in a ship called the Mayflower. *(lines 56–59)*
   - **a.** action
   - **b.** group
   - **c.** progress

9. The leaders strictly <u>ruled</u> the settlers according to their own fundamentalist Christian principles and displayed no toleration for any other religion, especially a Native American one. *(lines 68–70)*
   - **a.** lined
   - **b.** governed
   - **c.** decided

10. At best they were tolerated as naïve and primitive creatures; at worst, they were abused, enslaved, and slaughtered. Africans <u>fared</u> no better, of course. *(lines 80–82)*
    - **a.** experience
    - **b.** cost
    - **c.** transport

11. In contrast to the Puritans of Massachusetts, the Protestants of Rhode Island lived under a considerable <u>degree</u> of toleration for diverse cultures and faiths. *(lines 105–07)*
    - **a.** stage
    - **b.** grade
    - **c.** amount

POLITICAL SCIENCE

A. PARALLEL STRUCTURES AND ELLIPSES

When you first begin composing sentences in English, you probably think of a very simple sentence that includes one subject, one verb, and one object. However, the more exposure you have to academic English—the type of English you find in college textbooks—the more often you see very complex sentences with multiple clauses and parallel structures. Parallel structures are words or phrases that serve the same grammatical function, for example as subjects or as verbs. Often when there is information repeated in these structures, you can remove it. This is known as an ellipsis. For example:

Washington led the Continental Army and Washington became the first president of the US →

Washington led the Continental Army and ~~Washington~~ became the first president of the US →

Washington led the Continental Army and became the first president of the US

What you remove from the sentence in an ellipsis must be repeated or synonymous words or phrases, NOT new information. Ellipses can occur at different places in a sentence. Notice the parallel structures that are removed in the following sentences.

   a. *My father worked in a factory and ~~my father worked in~~ an office.*

   b. *Michelle studied nursing and ~~Michelle studied~~ business.*

   c. *This summer we should stay in town and ~~we should~~ save our money.*

   d. *Last year we traveled to New York and ~~to~~ Chicago.*

B. *In the following text, draw a line through any unnecessary parallel structures.*

George Washington is one of the most beloved and one of the most respected of the Founding Fathers of the United States of America. Comparable to men like Thomas Jefferson, Alexander Hamilton, and John Adams, Washington's role in establishing this nation was indeed immense. Washington was the leader of the Continental Army during the revolution and the leader of the nation after the revolution. He is deeply admired for his selfless efforts at protecting the country and at founding a democratic state. However, Washington was also eager to promote himself as a hero and Washington was eager to leave for posterity an image of himself as a very great man.

Moreover, George Washington was committed to expanding his material wealth. He worked to acquire vast tracts of land and to acquire hundreds of slaves, even though his feelings about slavery were ambivalent. Unlike other slave owners, Washington would not allow enslaved families to be split up and he would not allow them to be sent away from each other. Yet as a man of material desires, benefitting from the use of slave labor, he used stealth and he used deception in order to steal away a number of his slaves from Pennsylvania when that state was legislating to allow slaves their freedom. Washington instead had these slaves transported to Virginia, Washington's home state, where slavery remained quite legal. By removing his slaves from Pennsylvania and by bringing them to Virginia, Washington ensured that these slaves were not allowed to go free and were not permitted to pursue a new life in the very country that Washington had struggled to free from British control.

C. *Each of the following passages from the essay "Early American Democracy" includes a parallel structure with an ellipsis. Circle the correct choice to indicate what has been removed from these sentences.*

1. Both Athenian and American democracy were restricted by essentially undemocratic beliefs and practices. *(lines 6–8)*

    a. Both Athenian ~~democracy~~ and American democracy were restricted by essentially undemocratic beliefs and ~~undemocratic~~ practices.

    b. Both ~~the~~ Athenian and American democracy were restricted by essentially undemocratic beliefs and ~~unfair~~ practices

2. In these public meetings, people could express their opinions and negotiate decisions about public matters. *(lines 13–14)*

    a. In these public meetings, people could express their opinions and ~~people could~~ negotiate decisions about public matters.

    b. In these public meetings, people could express their opinions and ~~people in meetings could~~ negotiate decisions about public matters.

3. Many of these colonists were little more than treasure seekers, hoping to find gold and get rich quickly. *(lines 35–36)*

    a. Many of these colonists were little more than treasure seekers, hoping to find gold and ~~to~~ get rich quickly.

    b. Many of these colonists were little more than treasure seekers, hoping to find gold and ~~wanting to~~ get rich quickly.

4. They had little interest in building homes or cultivating crops. *(lines 36–37)*

    a. They had little interest in building homes and ~~they had~~ cultivating crops.

    b. They had little interest in building homes or ~~in~~ cultivating crops.

5. He quickly assessed that the colony needed discipline and required order. *(lines 43–44)*

    a. He quickly assessed that the colony needed discipline and ~~so he~~ required order.

    b. He quickly assessed that the colony needed discipline and ~~the colony~~ required order.

D. *There are more parallel structures in the essay that include ellipses. Find such sentences somewhere between the lines indicated below. Write them in the space provided below and include in parentheses the parallel structures that were removed from these sentences.*

1. *(lines 50–55)* _____

    _____

    _____

2. *(lines 55–60)* _____

    _____

3. *(lines 61–65)* _____

    _____

4. *(lines 99–104)* _____

    _____

    _____

POLITICAL SCIENCE   JOURNAL WRITING 4.2

Choose from the following options for your journal writing assignment:

1. European colonists in the Americas often clashed with the Native American communities they encountered here. For many years, Europeans denied citizenship to the natives of the Americas, perceiving them to be inferior to Europeans in nearly every way. Are there native or indigenous cultures in your home country? Write the names of as many indigenous cultures as you can.

    a. _____   e. _____   i. _____

    b. _____   f. _____   j. _____

    c. _____   g. _____   k. _____

    d. _____   h. _____   l. _____

    What do you know about them? How are native cultures distinct from other cultures? How are native people treated? Are they granted citizenship? Do they continue to speak their own native languages? Write about the interaction of native and non-native cultures in the United States or in your home country.

2. Roger Williams was a devout Christian who believed in the necessity of purifying the Christian Church. However, he also believed that the government should not involve itself in the religious affairs of the people. This secularist separation of church and state was later amended to the Constitution of the United States, but there are still arguments today over the separation of government and church. What do you think about this? Should the government promote a particular religion for the people of a country? Should it encourage people to live a more spiritual or religious life? Should religious instruction and time for prayer be included in schools? Or should there be a strict separation between the religious life of an individual and the non-religious work of governments and schools? Explain your reasoning.

3. The voyage from Europe to the Americas could last 2–3 months and was a very dangerous journey during which many people died. And yet millions of people eventually made that journey to begin a new life. People have left their home countries and come to the colonies and later to the United States for a variety of reasons. Begin this writing assignment by making a list of reasons why people leave their homes and travel to live somewhere else.

    a. _____

    b. _____

    c. _____

    d. _____

    e. _____

    Now write about this process of leaving one's home and beginning a new life elsewhere, using yourself as an example. What is this process like? Why did you come here? What challenges have you faced?

BIOLOGY

It is safe to assume that for as long as humans have walked the earth, we have been curious about life. The origin and nature and even the purpose of life have been discussed and debated and examined in literature and mythology and religion, just to name a few manifestations of human thought and expression. But what role have science and scientific research played in our understanding of life? While interest in life is quite ancient, the modern scientific field of biology is relatively young. Nonetheless, it has taught us much, and research in biology has had a deep impact on our understanding of medicine, anatomy, botany, zoology, physiology, and many other fields of study.

A. What do you know about biology? What information can you share with your group about the following concepts:

1. life and death _____

   _____

2. evolution of life _____

   _____

3. organs and organisms _____

   _____

4. cells _____

   _____

5. genes _____

   _____

B. Below are images that depict six distinct systems within the human body. Working with your group, compose a description of each system. What are the elements that make up each system? What purpose do these systems serve in maintaining human life? How are these systems different from those of a plant or a non-human animal?

Human Body Systems

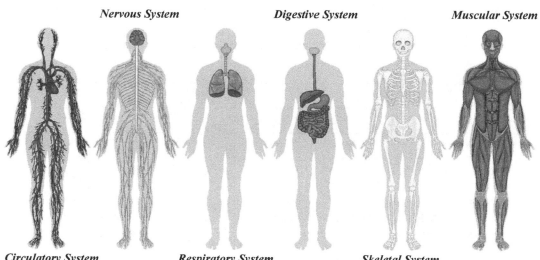

Nervous System   *Digestive System*   *Muscular System*

Circulatory System   *Respiratory System*   *Skeletal System*

BIOLOGY

A. *Using a dictionary to help you, circle the word in each row that is NOT a synonym for the highlighted vocabulary word.*

1. **compound**	simple	multiple	composite
2. **conclusion**	deduction	inference	initiation
3. **distinct**	different	discreet	similar
4. **evolution**	stasis	transformation	alteration
5. **identify**	determine	recognize	confuse
6. **microscopic**	tiny	macroscopic	imperceptible
7. **occur**	take place	happen	precede
8. **organism**	life form	being	concept
9. **perceive**	sense	overlook	discern
10. **prior**	subsequent	previous	preceding
11. **sequence**	interruption	succession	progression
12. **structure**	arrangement	framework	disorganization

B. *Write the letter of the correct synonym to match the meaning of the vocabulary words highlighted in the sentences below.*

1. _____ With the **conclusion** of the meeting, Rachel hurried off to the cafeteria to grab a coffee.

2. _____ You and I studied the same data in the same experiment. I don't see how you could reach the opposite **conclusion** from me.

3. _____ The judge's **conclusion** surprised everyone in the courtroom, especially the defendant, who was so sure he would be set free.

   a. decision

   b. deduction

   c. end

   d. finally

   e. termination

4. _____ Mimi's award for her outstanding academic achievement was a **distinct** honor.

5. _____ I stopped walking and listened carefully, and I was sure I had heard the **distinct** sound of laughter from across the street.

6. _____ We interpret the First Amendment to the Constitution as saying that *church* and *state* must be **distinct** from one another.

   f. clear

   g. definite

   h. different

   i. exceptional

   j. separate

C. **Certain prefixes describing size or number can be very common in scientific studies like biology. What do the following prefixes mean?**

micro- _____   *uni-* _____

macro- _____   *multi-* _____

Choose from the following terms to match the descriptions or definitions below.

microcosm	*macrocosm*	*unicellular*	*multicellular*
microcyst	*macrocyst*	*unidirectional*	*multidirectional*
microeconomics	*macroeconomics*	*unilateral*	*multilateral*
microevolution	*macroevolution*	*unilingual*	*multilingual*
microorganism	*macroorganism*	*uninucleate*	*multinucleate*
microscopic	*macroscopic*	*universe*	*multiverse*

1. _____ : the broader or more general aspects of a financial system

2. _____ : higher level changes when one organism transforms into another

3. _____ : flowing in a single bearing, such as north or south

4. _____ : a life form too small to be viewed by the naked eye

5. _____ : a small society of people perceived to represent all societies

6. _____ : comprehending and producing more than one language

7. _____ : with only a single nucleus, unlike cells with two or more nuclei

8. _____ : the combined total of all existing matter, including the universe

9. _____ : having only one side or decided by only one negotiating party

10. _____ : being composed of many cells, such as a human being

D. **Circle the vocabulary word that best completes each of the following sentences.**

1. Oscar's ability to learn languages is quite *compound / distinct / occur*. I have never seen a student learn English as quickly as he does.

2. Using an electron microscope, we can now *perceive / prior / structure* matter that is too small to appear under an optical microscope.

3. The more we study the animal kingdom, the more we can agree that there is no other *conclusion / evolution / organism* that is as creative as humans.

4. Your computer will only start up if you enter each letter and number of your password in the correct *sequence / compound / conclusion*.

5. I would say that your *prior / microscopic / distinct* essay was better written than your new paper, and that it was more interesting to read.

6. With this new blood test, we can accurately *occur / identify / perceive* the virus that is damaging your immune system.

Active reading can help you better understand a college text. Begin by discussing the questions below. Then carefully read the following essay, taking notes on the main points and important details that you find in the text. Also select the best meaning for words highlighted in the right-hand column.

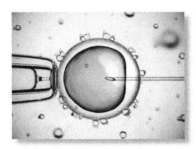

PREREADING DISCUSSION

1. What would you say all life is made of? What is it really that makes us alive? How does life come to an end?
2. What are cells? What are cells made of? Are there different types of cells? Can you describe them?
3. What differences and similarities are there between distinct types of organisms? How are humans different from other animals? How are animals different from plants?

(1)   Do you recall if you have ever looked through a *microscope*? There are several different types of microscope, but chances are you have either used or at least seen what is known as an *optical microscope*, which uses visible light and one or more lenses to expand or magnify the sample that you are examining. A

5   *simple microscope* uses one lens, much like a magnifying glass, while a *compound microscope* uses multiple lenses to collect the light from the sample and even more lenses to focus that light into the eye of the observer. Thanks to the optical microscope, humans can see things that are otherwise too small for the naked eye to perceive.

10   (2)   We do not know who actually invented the optical microscope, but its contribution to cellular biology cannot be exaggerated. In fact, the very term *cell* was first used by a man named Robert Hooke in a book he published in 1665 entitled *Micrographia*. For his observations, Hooke was using a compound optical microscope designed specifically for him

15   and constructed of leather and gold and of course, a very important system of lenses. Through these lenses, Hooke examined plants magnified to such an extent that he could see microscopic structures. These structures reminded him of the tiny cells in monasteries where monks would dwell, and so Hooke called them "cells."

Using an optical microscope

20   (3)   Hooke's conclusions from his observations were significant, yet quite minimal. He did not accurately perceive the structure of each cell, nor could he determine their function. All he had really perceived were the walls of cells and not the life that moves inside of them. The first person to peer inside a live cell through a microscope and actually witness what you might call the moving parts

25   of a cell was Anton van Leeuwenhoek. In 1674, Leeuwenhoek saw things moving inside a live cell of the algae Spirogyra and called them *animalcules* or "little animals." These discoveries begged the question—is the life of a complex organism somehow dependent on the lives of the "little animals" inside of them? In other words, am I alive today because I have living cells inside of me?

30   (4)   To any college student today, the answer to this question might seem almost absurdly simple. However, keep in mind that centuries ago, prior to the discovery of cells, a very different answer was favored in scientific and philosophical circles. Many people believed that a vital element distinguishes living organisms from lifeless objects—a spark of life or a soul, which inanimate

35   objects do not have. In effect, proponents of this theory of *vitalism* were arguing

line 27: beg the question

a. ask for a question
b. plead for something
c. necessitate inquiry

Another example:
Your insistence that you just cannot take the test today begs the question, "Why not?"

that we are alive, because we have life in us—not a particularly useful theory, and one which was rejected with a maximum of derision in the years to come as studies in cell biology progressed.

(5)   *Cell biology* is the discipline that studies all aspects of
40   cells: how they come into existence, how they live and die, their structure and function, what they contain inside, and the different types of cells known to exist. All cells can be divided into two basic types: *eukaryotes* (cells that contain a nucleus, pronounced *yū-kɛ'-ri-ōts*) and *prokaryotes* (cells that
45   contain no nucleus, pronounced *prō-kɛ'-ri-ōts*). These types of cells can be further subdivided according to their structure and function. So, for example, the human body possesses a number of disparate cells, including red blood cells, bone cells, and nerve cells. Each type is distinct from one another,
50   but they all have certain features in common. For instance, nearly all human cells have a nucleus, which means they are all eukaryotic cells.[11]

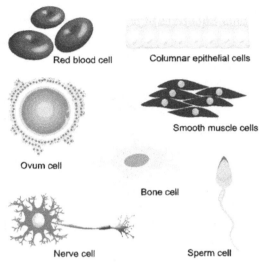

ANATOMY OF HUMAN CELLS

Red blood cell

Columnar epithelial cells

Smooth muscle cells

Ovum cell

Bone cell

Nerve cell

Sperm cell

(6)   *Prokaryotes*—organisms composed of prokaryotic cells—are relatively simple life forms. In fact, most
55   prokaryotes are unicellular (or single-celled) organisms, such as bacteria. In contrast, if you are reading this book, then you must belong to the very diverse family of *eukaryotes*, which includes plants, animals, fungi, and protists. *Protists* are microorganisms that constitute a distinct group of eukaryotes—different from other eukaryotes in that they can be
60   unicellular, but also multicellular without specialized *tissues* (groups of cells that work together to perform a specific function, such as nervous tissue or muscle tissue).

(7)   It is easy to determine which group of organisms humans belong to, because almost all cells
65   in the human body have a nucleus. Remember, the defining characteristic of eukaryotic cells is that they possess a nucleus along with other structures, known as *organelles* ("little organs"), which are also enclosed within membranes. The double membrane that
70   surrounds the nucleus of the cell is also referred to as the *nuclear envelope*. Most eukaryotic cells also contain other miniscule organelles, such as the *mitochondria* found in most eukaryotes and the *chloroplasts* found in plants and algae. As the name
75   "organelle" suggests, mitochondria and chloroplasts function as the organs of a cell. Chloroplasts trap energy from sunlight through the process of photosynthesis, while mitochondria are involved in a number of functions, most prominently the production
80   of energy for the cell.

Structure of a Typical Animal Cell

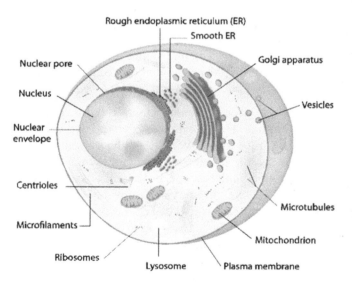

Rough endoplasmic reticulum (ER)

Smooth ER

Golgi apparatus

Nuclear pore

Nucleus

Vesicles

Nuclear envelope

Centrioles

Microtubules

Microfilaments

Mitochondrion

Ribosomes

Lysosome

Plasma membrane

(8)   However, what most clearly distinguishes eukaryotic cells from prokaryotic cells is the existence of a *nucleus*. Animal cells may possess multiple mitochondria. Plants cells may contain multiple chloroplasts. But all eukaryotic cells contain only one nucleus. And one is all you need. Think of it

85   this way—the nucleus is the information center of the cell, directing the cell how
to grow, how to work, how to repair itself. If there were more than one center,
the cell might not survive because of the mixed messages.

(9)   Those messages or instructions that govern the functioning of a cell are
90   encoded in the molecules of the cell's *DNA* (Deoxyribonucleic acid), which is
found in the chromosomes inside the nucleus[12]. All known forms of life require
nucleic acid, along with proteins and carbohydrates. DNA provides the genetic
instruction for all organisms and many viruses. Without DNA, cells could not
function properly—nor could they even grow or replicate to begin with. Human
life depends on one cell—a fertilized egg or *zygote*—dividing into two cells, and
95   these two cells dividing into four cells, and so on. Multicellular organisms
depend on cell division to grow and survive, and each cell division must replicate
the chromosomes in the nucleus of the original cell so that both new or *daughter
cells* now possess the same DNA. It may be that aging occurs because our cells
slowly lose the ability to correctly divide and replicate.

100   (10)   DNA was first discovered in Switzerland back in 1869. There,
physician Friedrich Miescher was using a microscope to examine what
was left on discarded bandages. Miescher noticed a microscopic
substance in the pus, which he named *nuclein*. Nine years later, Albrecht
Kossel identified the nucleic acid within Miescher's nuclein, along with
105   five bases, including the four bases that we now know construct the actual
genetic codes of DNA: *cytosine* (C), *guanine* (G), *adenine* (A), and
thymine (T). However, it was the work of James Watson and Francis
Crick in 1953 that produced the memorable double helix model of DNA,
work that earned them the Nobel Prize in 1962 along with Maurice
110   Wilkins.

(11)   So for growth to occur, cells must divide, and when cells divide
properly (in humans, through a process called *mitosis*), the DNA of the cell is
replicated. However, we cannot be certain whether your cells will divide
correctly or not. As you might expect from the replication of such an incredibly
115   complex code, problems can occur during cell division. After all, the genetic
code that was formed from your mother's egg and your father's sperm—which
together created your DNA—includes over three billion base pairs in a peculiar
sequence. In other words, your code consists of billions and billions of Cs and
Gs and As and Ts, all determining your height and skin tone and hair color and
120   how many arms you have and how many legs and eyes and so on. In many ways,
DNA identifies who you will become.

(12)   There are different types of problems that can occur during cell division.
Some minimal segments of the genetic code might be deleted. Others might be
incorrectly sequenced or replicated or even duplicated so that your body tries to
125   grow with too much code. These mutations do not seem to be as common as you
might expect, and our DNA has a built-in safety device that seeks to repair such
mistakes before they can do any real harm. Moreover, it is not entirely true that
genetic mutations are all bad. Evolutionary theory argues that some mutations
might prove beneficial to an organism—so beneficial in fact that its chances of
130   survival and procreation are increased, and thus the mutation may be passed on to
the children for generations to come. Species might evolve in part because of
successful genetic mutations.

---

line 105: base

a.   dishonorable
b.   compound
c.   foundation

Another example:
*Chemical bases are
capable of bonding with
an acid.*

*Illustration of the double helix
model of DNA*

---

line 117: peculiar

a.   strange
b.   individual
c.   particular

Another example:
*If we do not follow the
peculiar steps required in
making this dish, it will
not taste right.*

---

line 130: pass on

a.   to decline
b.   to share
c.   to die

Another example:
*I think my mother passed
on her love of food to me;
I just can't stop eating!*

A. *In some college textbooks, italic letters are used to identify new vocabulary or terms that you are expected to know. Skim through the reading "Cells: The Units of Life." Find the following italicized terms in the text and write the letter of the correct description or definition below for each term.*

1. _____ *adenine*

2. _____ *animalcules*

3. _____ *cell biology*

4. _____ *compound microscope*

5. _____ *DNA*

6. _____ *eukaryotes*

7. _____ *mitochondria*

8. _____ *nuclear envelope*

9. _____ *nucleus*

10. _____ *optical microscope*

11. _____ *organelles*

12. _____ *prokaryotes*

13. _____ *protists*

14. _____ *tissue*

15. _____ *vitalism*

16. _____ *zygote*

a. uses visible light to examine a sample

b. uses multiple lenses to view a sample

c. the "little animals" or living parts of a cell

d. belief that life depends on the spark of life or soul inside

e. the study of all aspects of cells

f. cells that contain a nucleus

g. cells that do not contain a nucleus

h. microorganisms that can be unicellular or multicellular

i. groups of cells that work together to perform a specific function

j. a little organ within a cell that has a specific function

k. the double membrane that surrounds the nucleus of a cell

l. organelles that provide energy for the cell

m. a special organelle that is also the information center of a cell

n. a nucleic acid that carries genetic code in the nucleus of a cell

o. a fertilized egg that divides into multiple cells to form life

p. one of the four bases that construct our genetic code

B. *Skim through the essay once again and write the name of the individual(s) associated with each of the following developments in the field of biology: Hooke, Leeuwenhoek, Miescher, or Watson & Crick.*

1. _____ : the first man to identify microscopic structures as cells

2. _____ : the man who discovered DNA

3. _____ : won the Nobel Prize in 1962

4. _____ : the first man to identify the parts of a living cell

5. _____ : authored the book *Micrographia* about his work using a microscope

6. _____ : produced the double-helix model of DNA

7. _____ : called the organelles of cells "little animals"

8. _____ : identified nuclein in the pus on discarded bandages

C. **Read the following statements. Do they agree with the information in the essay? Circle T (true) or F (false) for each statement.**

1.   T   F   Mitochondria use a process known as photosynthesis to trap energy in cells.

2.   T   F   Robert Hooke was the first man to view the living parts of a cell.

3.   T   F   Most cells in the human body are eukaryotic.

4.   T   F   Hooke used the term "cell" because what he saw under a microscope reminded him of the rooms in monasteries.

5.   T   F   The theory of vitalism was not based on an understanding of cells.

6.   T   F   Cell biology describes how all life depends on a spark of life within it.

7.   T   F   There are two basic types of cells: *eukaryotes* and *prokaryotes*.

8.   T   F   Mitochondria and chloroplasts serve the same basic function.

9.   T   F   Animal cells can have more than one mitochondrion.

10.   T   F   Hooke used a compound microscope to identify the cells of human skin tissue.

11.   T   F   All known forms of life require nucleic acid, protein, and carbohydrates.

12.   T   F   Every cell in the human body is actually an organelle serving a function.

13.   T   F   DNA provides the genetic instruction for all organisms.

14.   T   F   Friedrich Miescher discovered DNA while examining pus under a microscope.

15.   T   F   Albrecht Kossel identified the five bases that construct our genetic code.

D. **Look at the following illustration of a human cell. Can you fill in the missing names of the parts of the cell?**

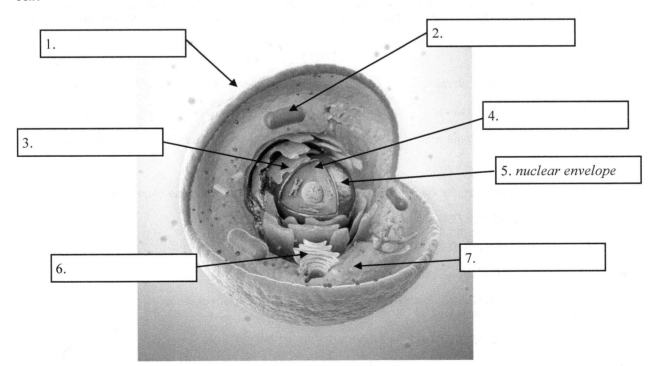

BIOLOGY

A. THE FORM AND FUNCTION OF NOUN CLAUSES

We often think of a sentence as a clause containing three parts: SUBJECT and VERB and PREDICATE. In a simple sentence, the SUBJECT and the PREDICATE might be a pronoun or a noun or a noun phrase. For example,

	SUBJECT	VERB	PRONOUN as PREDICATE
I didn't know it. →	I	didn't know	it.

	SUBJECT	VERB	NOUN PHRASE as PREDICATE
I didn't know his name. →	I	didn't know	his name.

However, sometimes we need to say more than just a noun or noun phrase. The SUBJECT or PREDICATE of a sentence might be an entire clause with its own SUBJECT, VERB, and PREDICATE. For example,

	SUBJECT	VERB	NOUN CLAUSE as PREDICATE
1. I didn't know what his name was. →	I	didn't know	what his name was.
2. I didn't know if you were coming with us. →	I	didn't know	if you were coming with us.
3. I didn't know that there was a test today. →	I	didn't know	that there was a test today.

B. In the three examples above, you can see the three different types of NOUN CLAUSES based on the kind of question or statement that is used as the SUBJECT or PREDICATE of the simple independent clause.

		COMBINING CLAUSES	TYPE OF NOUN CLAUSE
1.	I didn't know what his name was. →	I didn't know + What was his name?	wh- question
2.	I didn't know if you were coming with us. →	I didn't know + Were you coming with us?	yes-no question
3.	I didn't know that there was a test today. →	I didn't know + There was a test today.	statement

Notice how questions do not keep the **question word order** *when they become noun clauses:*

WHY ARE YOU LATE? → Tell me WHY YOU ARE LATE.

Moreover, the helping verb **do/does/did** *is NOT used in question noun clauses:*

WHEN DID SHE CALL? → Do you know WHEN SHE CALLED?

Finally, while NOUN CLAUSES are often used as predicates, especially in academic texts, they can function as **subjects** *of sentences as well:*

HOW DID THE FIRE START? → HOW THE FIRE STARTED is still unknown.

C. *Below are eleven sentences from the essay "Cells: The Units of Life." Underline the noun clause in each sentence. If the noun clause was formed from a question, then rewrite the noun clause as a question. For example:*

> ### *Have you heard <u>if Samantha is coming to the party</u>?*
>
> **QUESTION**:   *Is Samantha coming to the party?*

1. Do you recall if you have ever looked through a microscope? *(line 1)*

    QUESTION: _____

2. Chances are you have either used or at least seen what is known as an optical microscope. *(lines 2–3)*

    QUESTION: _____

3. We do not know who actually invented the optical microscope. *(line 10)*

    QUESTION: _____

4. Many people believed that a vital element distinguishes living organisms from lifeless objects. *(lines 33–34)*

    QUESTION: _____

5. Proponents of this theory of *vitalism* were arguing that we are alive. *(lines 35–36)*

    QUESTION: _____

6. It is easy to determine which group of organisms humans belong to. *(lines 63–64)*

    QUESTION: _____

7. The defining characteristic of eukaryotic cells is that they possess a nucleus. *(lines 65–67)*

    QUESTION: _____

8. Friedrich Miescher was using a microscope to examine what was left on discarded bandages. *(lines 101–02)*

    QUESTION: _____

9. We cannot be certain whether your cells will divide correctly or not. *(lines 113–14)*

    QUESTION: _____

10. In many ways, DNA identifies who you will become. *(lines 120–21)*

    QUESTION: _____

11. Evolutionary theory argues that some mutations might prove beneficial to an organism. *(lines 128–29)*

    QUESTION: _____

D. Complete the following text about hair color and genetics by circling the word that most likely introduces the noun clause in each sentence.

Have you ever wondered **(1)** *when / why / that* you look the way you do? Research in genetics tells us **(2)** *that / if / where* our physical appearance is largely determined by the DNA we inherit from our mothers and fathers. However, we cannot say **(3)** *that / how / which* parent gives us our eye color or our hair color. The truth is **(4)** *that / whether / who* both parents contribute equally to our genetic makeup. And yet, you may be able to guess **(5)** *whether / when / who* your mother or your father played the dominant role in your hair color by looking at their own families. Let's say **(6)** *which / that / if* you have dark brown hair. Ask your parents **(7)** *if / how / when* brown hair is dominant in their families. Have you noticed **(8)** *who / when / how* one color of hair seems to dominate most members of a family? If your mother's family have different colors of hair—some brown, some blond, some auburn—but nearly everyone in your father's family have dark brown hair, then we can argue **(9)** *whether / where / that* your father's genes for hair color were dominant in your DNA.

E. Complete the following dialogues by rewriting the sentence that person A says as a noun clause in the response given by person B.

1.   A: Which road should I take to get to the store?

       B: How should I know _____

2.   A: Our favorite café has shut down.

       B: I didn't know _____

3.   A: How long will the test last?

       B: The teacher has not said _____

4.   A: I have decided to study medicine.

       B: We are very happy _____

5.   A: Is Carla staying for dinner?

       B: I don't know _____

6.   A: Why did the prime minister resign his position?

       B: They haven't said _____

7.   A: Are we all meeting after class?

       B: I have not heard _____

8.   A: The new law will go into effect next month.

       B: Really? Did the government say _____

9.   A: Is Oscar ready for the test?

       B: I really doubt _____

BIOLOGY

Earlier we discussed the question of differences between humans and other animals. For this writing assignment, begin by completing the chart below with some relevant differences or similarities between humans, dogs, fish, and plants.

humans	*dogs*	*fish*	*plants*

Now use the information in this chart to write a paper that focuses on one of the following themes:

1. How special are we as human beings? What are the qualities or characteristics that you think separate humans from other forms of life? What are humans capable of doing that other animals cannot do? What would you say are the greatest accomplishments of human kind?

2. How are humans part of the animal kingdom? What do we share in common with other mammals, such as dogs or chimps? How are we close to other kinds of animals? Are there any animals that you feel more comfortable with? Are there any animals that you admire? Or fear? Why do you think that is?

3. How does life change? The argument for evolution in living creatures suggests that the origin of all life can be traced back to the simplest single-celled organisms billions of years ago. Can you see anything in humans that might link them to a long process of evolution or change from some other kind of creature?

BIOLOGY   VOCABULARY 5.2

A. Here are our target vocabulary for Reading 2 in this unit:

analyze	emphasize	process	scripture
compel	interpretation	promote	theory
constant	observation	propose	variation

B. When you learn a new verb, such as IDENTIFY, try also to learn which objects are likely to be associated with that verb. For example, as a student of Biology, you might be asked to IDENTIFY many things, including an ORGANISM, a SPECIES, or a VIRUS. Look at the following highlighted verbs, which are based on words in our vocabulary list. Each verb is followed by three objects. Circle the two objects that are most likely to be associated with the verb.

1. **analyze**	data	a problem	furniture
2. **emphasize**	a virus	a point	a word
3. **interpret**	a dream	poetry	a garden
4. **observe**	behavior	an account	people
5. **promote**	a product	world peace	an organism
6. **propose**	an idea	an actress	a solution

C. The word "scripture" is a form of the word "script," which derives from a Latin word related to the idea of "writing." Each of the following sentences describes a word that is related to "script." Match the correct words to the sentences and underline words or phrases in the sentence that helped you make your guess.

a. conscript	*c. indescribable*	*e. prescription*	*g. scribe*	*i. scripture*
b. describe	*d. inscription*	*f. proscribe*	*h. script*	*j. scriptwriter*

1. _____ Teachers have decided to prohibit the use of mobile phones in the classroom, because such devices distract students from learning and are easily used for cheating.

2. _____ Charles is such a great storyteller. I was not at all surprised to hear that he now writes screenplays for movies.

3. _____ With his name written on the list of soldiers, Mehmet had no choice but to join the army.

4. _____ The text written into the Rosetta Stone enabled Champollion to decipher hieroglyphics.

5. _____ Before you can pick up your medicine, you need a note from your doctor.

6. _____ Our trip to Paris was so incredible, I cannot find the words to tell you about it.

7. _____ The writings of the Old Testament include far more than just ten commandments.

8. _____ The history of ancient China was recorded by men who were experts in the Chinese writing system.

D. **When you learn new vocabulary, take the time to consider the different forms of those words. How would you write the different parts of speech for the following vocabulary words? Use a dictionary to help you complete the chart below. Some forms of the words do not exist or are unnecessary to complete the chart.**

	VERB	*NOUN*	*ADJECTIVE*	*ADVERB*
1.	analyze			analytically
2.	compel		compelling	
3.	emphasize			emphatically
4.		interpretation		
5.		observation		
6.	promote		promotional	
7.	propose			
8.		theory		theoretically
9.		variation	varying	

E. **Look again at the nine groups of words in Part D. Choose two words each from four of those groups and write sentences with them. For example:**

    a. *The president has compelled Congress to consider a new environmental law.*

    b. *There is compelling evidence that the climate is indeed changing.*

1.   a. _____

       _____

      b. _____

       _____

2.   a. _____

       _____

      b. _____

       _____

3.   a. _____

       _____

      b. _____

       _____

4.   a. _____

       _____

      b. _____

       _____

BIOLOGY

Discuss the questions below with your peers. Then carefully read the following essay on "Evolution: How Life Changes," taking notes on the main points and important details, figures, and events that you find in the text. Also select the best meaning for words highlighted in the right-hand column.

PREREADING DISCUSSION

1. Who was Charles Darwin? What do you know about him? What was his profession? What theory did he promote?
2. What is the theory of evolution all about? What does it suggest about life and how life changes? What kind of organisms might change according to this theory?
3. Do you think that humans can evolve? How have we changed? Where does your understanding of humans come from? Culture? School? Religion? Your own ideas?

(1)   Students of philosophy are very likely to be familiar with the names of Socrates, Plato, and Aristotle. Aristotle (384–322 BC) was not just a brilliant philosopher, but a naturalist—a man who studied the natural world. Aristotle was also determined to derive laws of nature from his observations. In fact, to
5   understand humans, he argued, we must understand the natural world to which humans belong. And the world of nature is a world of change. However, Aristotle was not the first to propose this idea of change in nature. A century and a half before Aristotle's observations, another philosopher—Heraclitus—argued that "Nothing endures but change." Change is the only constant.

10   (2)   It is difficult to argue with a statement like that, and yet humans seem uncomfortable with living in a universe that is in a constant state of flux. Human psychology is such that we derive comfort from things that are certain and unchanging. We need truths—or at the very least, ideas that we can believe are true. Constants promote a sense of security and stability, a sense that we know
15   what is happening around us today and can predict what will happen to tomorrow. One of the most debilitating psychoses is schizophrenia, which is characterized by a lack of historicity. In other words, for schizophrenic patients it is challenging to remember what has happened before in terms of their personal history and relationships, which makes it very hard to predict what will happen
20   next. And that is a very frightening thing for human beings.

(3)   What has remained a frightening and disturbing idea for many people today is the notion that humans themselves have been changing or evolving. Just hearing the term "evolution" causes some people to roll their eyes in frustration, muttering something like, "Oh, here we go again with those crazy ideas of
25   Darwin about humans evolving from monkeys!" However, the theory of evolution is about much more than just change in humans, and no proponent of evolution has ever argued that humans come from monkeys. As the great paleoanthropologist Louis Leakey (1903–1972) once wrote,

30   *People will stand in front of a chimpanzee in a zoo, or a stuffed gorilla in a museum, and say: 'I just could not believe that I am descended from that!' Scientists do not believe it either, nor do they ask someone else to believe it; but they do claim that the great apes and man had a common ancestor long ago. (Adam's Ancestors, 159)*

35   (4)   Moreover, the concept that life evolves—including human life—has been with us for millennia. Anaximander—another precursor of Aristotle—

> **line 11: state**
>
> **a.** province
> **b.** condition
> **c.** time
>
> **Another example:**
> *When the car hit me, I was in such a state of shock that I could not think straight.*

Chimpanzee

102

argued in the sixth century BC that humans had somehow evolved from fish. Some 2,000 years later, another group of thinkers were proposing their own theories of human and natural change. They came to be known as transformists, because at the heart of their beliefs was the principle that life transforms or
40   evolves over time from one form or species to another.

(5)   Evidence of this transformation was not to be found in genetic studies, of course, as we are talking about theories proposed several centuries ago, before genetic research really came into its own. However, there was certainly evidence of change to be found—an abundance of evidence in the very world around us.
45   And a man who excelled at observing and analyzing the natural world was a geologist from Scotland named Charles Lyell (1797–1875).

(6)   Lyell was inspired to pursue studies in geology by the preeminent geologist and paleontologist William Buckland (1784–1856). Buckland was not only the first researcher to write a full account of a dinosaur fossil; he was also a
50   reverend, and he was very keen on bridging the widening gap between science and faith. In fact, the term "gap" is quite appropriately used in reference to William Buckland since he initiated the idea that the Bible can fully account for all of natural history … so long as we are willing to reinterpret the gaps in the biblical narrative. In other words, the odd things that a geologist or
55   paleontologist discovers in the earth—such as dinosaur bones—belong to the gaps in history mentioned in scripture, but not fully explained by the Bible. Yes, Buckland would argue, dinosaurs too were part of God's creation, but they were wiped out in one of the catastrophes mentioned in the Bible, like the great flood. It was during such catastrophes that changes occurred over the earth.

60   (7)   Charles Lyell disagreed. He felt that Buckland and others were trying to compel the natural world to fit into their interpretations of scripture, even though the natural world explains itself well enough. Lyell insisted that common observable geological processes are quite enough to explain changes in the world around us, processes such as
65   rainfall and erosion and earthquakes and volcanoes. Furthermore, these processes have been influencing the shape of the world around us from beginning to end. Based on his geological observations, Lyell was the first to argue that natural history incorporates over 300 million years. In contrast, most people were inclined to follow the
70   preaching of Archbishop James Ussher (1581–1656) that the world —and all of creation!—was no more than about 6,000 years old.

(8)   Ussher's voice was one of many that promoted a reliance on scripture to understand the natural world. And it was from scripture that the monogenists derived their evidence that all of human kind shares a single origin,
75   as the name suggests: *mono + genesis*. The more religious monogenists of the 18th-20th centuries argued that the unique origin for all human kind was the first couple—Adam and Eve. However, if we all descended from one couple, then how can we understand variation in the human species? Why do there seem to be different races around the world with distinct skin color or facial features?

80   (9)   To answer this question, some monogenists emphasized following biblical interpretations. For example, in certain Protestant churches of the 18th and 19th centuries and within the early LDS church, a belief was promoted that dark or black skin was the physical mark that indicated the curse of Cain. The

Sir Charles Lyell.

Dinosaur fossils

---

line 36: argue

a.   contend
b.   dispute
c.   battle

Another example:
I argue that all students should be required to learn at least two languages.

---

line 77: descend

a.   go down
b.   come from
c.   fall over

Another example:
His family descend from the earliest European settlers in the Americas.

85 Bible does not say that Cain or his descendants were cursed with dark skin; only that Cain, the firstborn son of Adam and Eve, killed his brother Abel and was therefore cursed for his sin and that he bore the mark of this curse. For some monogenists, variation in skin color was thus explained by biblical events. However, other monogenists were more like William Buckland. They sought to wed the Bible to scientific discovery and claimed that variation in skin color was

90 due to climate and geography as well as to biblical events.

(10)   Emphasis on the Bible and faith played an important role in influencing early theories about humans and the natural world, even in some researchers who have been unfairly characterized as highly antireligious. The man whose name has become synonymous with "evolution" was far from hostile towards religion.

95 In fact, in his early years Charles Darwin was praised for his knowledge of scripture. He excelled in theological studies at Christ College in Cambridge and was thought to be a spiritual man who perceived divine design in the natural world around him.

(11)   Charles Darwin was born on 12 February 1809 in Shrewsbury, England

100 to a wealthy society doctor, Robert Darwin, and his wife Susannah, who died when Darwin was only eight years old. In 1825, after assisting his father in providing medical care to those in need, Darwin entered Edinburgh University to pursue studies in medicine. However, he was ill-suited to the subject, at least to surgery, which he found to be brutal and destructive. Instead, in his second year

105 at the university, he became interested in studying the natural world in general, and in particular the life cycle of marine animals, as a naturalist and geologist.

(12)   Darwin's principle theories were developed consequent to his five year voyage (1831–36) aboard the *HMS Beagle*, a voyage that allowed him to witness firsthand the incredible biological diversity of the natural world. During this

110 journey, Darwin spent a considerable amount of time on shore, studying marine life, geological features of the land, fossils both minute and gigantic, and the people he encountered. For Darwin, this was a life-altering experience. He analyzed innumerable species and contemplated all that he had observed.

(13)   In his journal Darwin explained the variations and distributions of

115 species according to the ideas of Charles Lyell. Indeed, Lyell's *Principles of Geology* was a constant companion to Darwin on the voyage. Once back in England, he continued to analyze the "species question." He was influenced in this by the economist Thomas Malthus, who observed that most living creatures produce far more offspring than could be expected to survive and reproduce.

120 Darwin argued that, in that case, there must be something about those that do survive which enables them to do so, some qualities or characteristics that increase their reproductive success. The capacity for such creatures to be selected for reproductive success he termed "natural selection."

(14)   Darwin realized that, if this theory were true, then the increasing

125 evidence argued not only that some individuals failed to reproduce, and that some species died out, but that surviving species could be said to have evolved over time as their innate characteristics were passed on to successive generations, which were in turn influenced by newer characteristics. Living organisms, in other words, were not created in their current form, as religious leaders argued,

130 but had evolved into this form from earlier forms. And if that were true of other creatures, then why not of man?

line 88: sought

a. *tried*
b. *looked for*
c. *followed*

Another example:
She sought to complete her degree in just two years.

Charles Darwin.

line 111: minute

a. *trivial*
b. *60 seconds*
c. *small*

Another example:
There is only a minute difference between these two species.

BIOLOGY

A. Which of the following statements best expresses the main point that the writer of "Evolution: How Life Changes" is trying to make?

1. The theory of biological change known as evolution falsely associates human beings with other animals, such as monkeys and chimpanzees.

2. The belief in change as a constant in the natural world has been promoted by researchers for millennia, including men like Aristotle, Charles Lyell, and Charles Darwin.

3. The Bible has long been a traditional source for understanding human origins and the natural world, including the identity of the first human couple—Adam and Eve.

B. As you were reading the essay, did you pay attention to the different professions that were mentioned? Draw lines to match each of the following professionals with what they might study.

1.	archbishop	a.	production, distribution, and consumption of goods and services
2.	economist	b.	ethics, metaphysics, and logic
3.	geologist	c.	origins and predecessors of the human species
4.	naturalist	d.	scripture, Latin, and church doctrine
5.	paleoanthropologist	e.	fossilized remains of early forms of life
6.	paleontologist	f.	physical, chemical, and biological changes of the earth
7.	philosopher	g.	plants, minerals, and animals of the natural world

C. Read through the essay once again and write the letter of each of the individuals below who were associated with the following fields, theories, or discoveries.

a. Aristotle	*c. Anaximander*	*e. William Buckland*	*g. James Ussher*
b. Heraclitus	*d. Charles Lyell*	*f. Charles Darwin*	*h. Thomas Malthus*

1. _____ believed that change is a natural aspect of life.
2. _____ was a naturalist.
3. _____ proposed the theory of *natural selection*.
4. _____ argued in favor of evolution.
5. _____ conducted research in geology.
6. _____ studied in Scotland.
7. _____ was a philosopher.
8. _____ had experience in the field of medicine.
9. _____ was educated in theology.
10. _____ studied dinosaur fossils.
11. _____ tried to find truth through scripture and science.
12. _____ wrote about issues of reproduction and survival.

D. Circle the letter of the best option to complete the sentences below based on your reading of the essay.

1. Aristotle tried to understand the world around him by observing _____
   a. ideas
   b. nature
   c. people

2. Schizophrenic patients have a hard time remembering _____
   a. scientific facts
   b. violent dreams
   c. personal history

3. Louis Leakey argued that humans and apes descended from _____
   a. Adam and Eve
   b. monkeys
   c. a common ancestor

4. Anaximander believed that humans had evolved from _____
   a. fish
   b. gods
   c. chimpanzees

5. William Buckland was the first to compose a complete description of _____
   a. human evolution
   b. a dinosaur fossil
   c. geological change

6. Buckland believed that dinosaurs _____
   a. were fully explained in the Bible, but that people have a hard time correctly interpreting scripture
   b. were not mentioned in the Bible because they never existed
   c. were not mentioned in the Bible but were destroyed by events described in the Bible

7. James Ussher believed that the world is no more than 6,000 years old based on his understanding of _____
   a. scripture
   b. evolution
   c. geology

8. Some religious groups have argued that dark skin derives from _____
   a. greater exposure to the sun
   b. an African origin for early humans
   c. a curse described in the scriptures

9. Charles Darwin abandoned his medical studies because he felt that surgery was too _____
   a. difficult
   b. dangerous
   c. destructive

10. During his voyage on the *HMS Beagle*, Darwin saw abundant evidence for _____ in the natural world.
    a. biological diversity
    b. divine creation
    c. human evolution

11. According to his theory of *natural selection*, Darwin argued that living organisms today _____
    a. have survived by killing off their competition
    b. exist in the form in which they were created
    c. have evolved while passing on characteristics to their children that help them to survive

BIOLOGY

A. COMPARING INFINITIVES AND GERUNDS

Look at the following sentences. Is there any difference in their meaning?

1.   **a.** *To learn a new language is very difficult.*
     b. *Learning a new language is very difficult.*

2.   **a.** *Maria continued to practice the piano until she was 20 years old.*
     b. *Maria continued practicing the piano until she was 20 years old.*

Sometimes there is no difference in meaning between the infinitive form of a verb [to VERB] and the gerund [VERBing]. Sentences (a) and (b) in number (1) and in number (2) mean the same thing. However, there may be a subtle difference in the individual style of the language user or in the context in which the language is used. For example, for some writers, it may feel more appropriate to use the INFINITIVE, because it sounds a little more formal, while informal speakers may prefer to use the GERUND. The meaning is the same, but the context is different.

With some verbs, there is a clear difference in meaning between the infinitive and the gerund:

3.   **a.** *Kathy stopped to study her homework.* =
        Kathy was doing something else, but then she stopped it so that she could study her homework.
     b. *Kathy stopped studying her homework.* =
        Kathy was studying her homework, but then she stopped studying.

4.   **a.** *I remembered to lock the door before I left.* =
        Before I left, I locked the door. I did not forget to do so.
     b. *I remembered locking the door before I left.* =
        I had a memory that I had locked the door before leaving.

B. Compare the following sentences. Circle SAME if the meaning is the same or DIFFERENT if the meaning has changed between the two sentences.

1.   **a.** *Matt forgot to bring his textbook to class.*   *SAME*   *DIFFERENT*
     b. *Matt forgot bringing his textbook to class.*

2.   **a.** *Nguyen loves to go shopping after school.*   *SAME*   *DIFFERENT*
     b. *Nguyen loves going shopping after school.*

3.   **a.** *He tried to run a marathon, but couldn't finish.*   *SAME*   *DIFFERENT*
     b. *He tried running a marathon, but couldn't finish.*

4.   **a.** *You should really start to go to bed early.*   *SAME*   *DIFFERENT*
     b. *You should really start going to bed early.*

5.   **a.** *Harry stopped to go to college when he was 30.*   *SAME*   *DIFFERENT*
     b. *Harry stopped going college when he was 30.*

C. **Some VERBS require either the INFINITIVE form of the verb or the GERUND, but will not allow you to use both. Underline the infinitives and gerunds in the sentences below. Then circle the verb that precedes each infinitive or gerund.**

1. Patty dislikes taking the bus to school, because she has to wait so long for it to arrive.

2. The police reported finding the gun in the ally after the robbery.

3. Bryan needs to spend more time on his homework if he wants to pass this class.

4. We decided to delay our trip until July when the weather is better.

5. You mentioned studying together this Friday. Are you still interested?

6. I tend to sleep in kind of late on the weekend after such a hard week of work.

7. Osman demonstrated playing the flute to his classmates during his presentation.

8. Michelle achieved finishing the test without a single mistake.

9. I'm sure you will do well in French, because you practice speaking it all the time.

10. Marcos was compelled to find a second job when he could not pay all his bills on time.

D. **Each of the following sentences from the essay "Evolution: How Life Changes" includes one or more infinitives or gerunds. Underline the infinitives or gerunds you find.**

1. Students of philosophy are very likely to be familiar with the names of Socrates, Plato, and Aristotle. *(lines 1–2)*

2. Aristotle was also determined to derive laws of nature from his observations. *(lines 3–4)*

3. It is difficult to argue with a statement like that, and yet humans seem uncomfortable with living in a universe that is in a constant state of flux. *(lines 10–11)*

4. For schizophrenic patients it is challenging to remember what has happened before in terms of their personal history and relationships, which makes it very hard to predict what will happen next. *(line 17–20)*

5. Just hearing the term "evolution" causes some people to roll their eyes in frustration. *(lines 22–24)*

6. And a man who excelled at observing and analyzing the natural world was a geologist from Scotland named Charles Lyell (1797–1875). *(lines 45–46)*

7. Buckland was not only the first researcher to write a full account of a dinosaur fossil; he was also a reverend, and he was very keen on bridging the widening gap between science and faith. *(lines 48–51)*

8. Ussher's voice was one of many that promoted a reliance on scripture to understand the natural world. *(lines 72–73)*

9. To answer this question, some monogenists emphasized following biblical interpretations. *(lines 80–81)*

10. Once back in England, he continued to analyze the "species question." *(lines 116–17)*

E.   When we describe what people think or how they feel, we often use ADJECTIVES followed by INFINITIVES. Can you identify them in these example sentences?

    a. *I am so eager to go on vacation. This has been a really tough semester.*

    b. *Even though he was nervous about his new job, Piero was pleased to meet his coworkers.*

    c. *Carmen was shocked to learn that her application to the university had been rejected.*

    d. *Remember, you should be careful to answer all the questions on the exam.*

    e. *I was very sad to hear about the loss of your father. Please accept my condolences.*

In a few cases, the infinitive and the gerund can mean the SAME thing after an adjective. For example, if Ben asks Moyad to play football with him and his friends, Moyad might say:

    a. *No thanks, I'm just happy to watch you guys play.*

    b. *No thanks, I'm just happy watching you guys play.*

F.   Complete the following sentences by writing the verb in parentheses in the INFINITIVE or GERUND form. If either form is possible, then write the form that feels most appropriate to you, but put a check by your answer to indicate that both forms are correct. Look again at the sentences in Parts A–E if you need help figuring out the correct answer.

1.   The bad weather caused us _____ *(miss)* our flight to Denver.

2.   Martha really dislikes _____ *(wait)* for the bus after school.

3.   Ruben continued _____ *(watch)* the movie until the end, even though he really didn't like it.

4.   Carver was shocked _____ *(receive)* a letter in the mail stating that he had lost his job. Nobody had even warned him about this happening.

5.   Nidia achieved _____ *(learn)* three languages at the same time.

6.   As a college student, you are likely _____ *(write)* many compositions.

7.   I am so happy _____ *(spend)* my time with you here.

8.   Karla is so good at basketball because she practices _____ *(play)* basketball two or three hours every day.

9.   What classes have you decided _____ *(take)* next semester?

10. I finally stopped _____ *(study)* at about 2:00 a.m. last night, because I was just too tired to continue.

11. My instructor emphasized _____ *(listen)* to news reports.

12. Believe me, it is difficult _____ *(find)* a true friend these days.

BIOLOGY

Choose from the following options for your journal writing assignment:

1. While some people might be inclined to think of science as a modern method of learning, scientific study has been with us for as long as humans have taken the time to observe and to manipulate the world around them in order to understand that world. Use whatever resources you need to—your peers, your library, the Internet—to find the names of six scientists from around the world. Write their names below.

   a. _____   d. _____

   b. _____   e. _____

   c. _____   f. _____

   Now that you have read a bit about these six people, which one is the most interesting to you? Write a paper describing one of these scientists and what he or she has accomplished with their studies.

2. While Charles Darwin is best remembered for his scientific studies and his advancement of the theory of evolution, his early education influenced him with a more traditional, religious approach to understanding the world around him. He felt that God provided man with a necessary sense of order and morality. After his voyage on the Beagle, he came to the conclusion that all life—including humans—must evolve. However, he was very hesitant about sharing his views with others, because he knew how deeply they would dislike what he had to say. Choose from one of the following for your journal writing assignment:

   a. Where does your understanding of the world come from? What guides you to see the natural world and the humans who live here in the way that you do? Do you depend on religion to answer questions for you? On some form of spirituality? On science? On your own observations? On the teachings of others that you have learned? Why do you believe the things that you do?

   b. Like Charles Darwin, the Russian physiologist Ivan Pavlov was initially educated in theology and was expected to work for the church. However, his later studies convinced him to stay away from religious teachings and depend more on a scientific approach to understanding truth. Have you ever faced such a conflict of belief before? Describe how your views have changed about what is right and true.

   c. Darwin was afraid to tell people he knew about his belief in evolution, including human evolution. Have you ever had to reveal something to others that you were afraid to share? What caused your fear? Were you afraid that people would not like you anymore? Would not trust you? Were you afraid that people would no longer want to be with the person you were becoming?

   d. One very important reason why Charles Darwin eventually shared his beliefs with others and continued to write even about human evolution was that other people encouraged him to do so. Thomas Huxley, for example, urged Darwin to continue his studies and publications because he believed in what Darwin was trying to say. Describe someone who has influenced you by urging you to believe in yourself. What was the result of this encouragement?

ASTRONOMY

One of the oldest known efforts of humans to scientifically observe and understand something beyond the self, astronomy is the study of all celestial objects, including planets and their satellites, such as our moon, as well as stars and the immense galaxies that are made of stars and planets, the remains of stars, and the dust and gas and dark matter in between.

A. Working with your peers, see how many of these questions you can answer about the universe we live in:

1. How many earths would fit inside our sun?
   - **a.** 42
   - **b.** 6,500
   - **c.** 1,300,000

2. What is the difference between a star and a sun?
   - **a.** A sun and a star are the same thing.
   - **b.** A sun is a star that has planets circling around it.
   - **c.** A star is bigger than a sun.

3. How many suns are there in our own Milky Way Galaxy?
   - **a.** 300 suns
   - **b.** 45,000 suns
   - **c.** 200,000,000,000 suns

4. Approximately how old is the universe?
   - **a.** 5,000 years old
   - **b.** 15,500,000 years old
   - **c.** 15,000,000,000 years old

5. What are the lights we see in the night sky?
   - **a.** stars and planets and galaxies
   - **b.** stars and planets
   - **c.** stars

B. Look at this image of our solar system. Can you identify and describe each of the planets?

ASTRONOMY   VOCABULARY 6.1

A. *Here are our target vocabulary for Reading 1 in this unit:*

appropriate	detect	phenomenon	predict
celestial	furthermore	potential	specific
circumstance	omen	precisely	visible

B. *Some root words in English are close enough in sound to simple existing words that you can fairly easily determine the meaning. If you had to guess, for example, what would you say the meaning of "circum-" is in a word like "circumstance"?*

clear   hope   reason   circle   quality

Match each of the following words with "circum-" to its most appropriate definition.

1. circumcise
2. circumference
3. circumflex
4. circumlocution
5. circumnavigate
6. circumpolar
7. circumscribe
8. circumspection
9. circumstance
10. circumvent

a. Caution about what someone should do.

b. The complete length of a circle.

c. Speaking around a subject rather than talking directly about it.

d. A mark over a letter often indicating a rounder sound.

e. Traveling around a pole of the earth.

f. To remove the foreskin of the penis, often for religious purposes.

g. To draw a line around something.

h. The conditions around you when something happens.

i. To go around or bypass an obstacle or requirement.

j. To fly or sail around the earth.

C. *Below are sentences from our next essay "Stars of the Ancients." Circle synonyms in the sentences for the highlighted vocabulary words.*

1. By conducting the ritual of sacrifice at the **appropriate** time with the moon, let's say, in its proper place, humans can recognize and celebrate the very order of the universe established by divinity.

2. The timely rise of a new moon, for instance, might enable you to **predict** victory in battle or to foresee defeat from the premature rise of a new moon.

3. The same text that records the movements of Venus also describes some 7,000 specific **omens**— signs of things that could happen depending on where the celestial bodies happen to be at any moment.

D.   Choose from the vocabulary words to complete the passage below.

In February 1633, Galileo Galilei arrived in Rome and appeared before Vincenzo Maculani, an *inquisitor* of the Roman Catholic Church. For any man to appear before the *Inquisition* was a terrible and frightening _____ (1). The _____ (2) of the Inquisition and its incidents of torture led to the deaths of thousands of people. It was the duty of the inquisitors, like Maculani, to _____ (3) sinful and sacrilegious behavior in Catholic lands and to punish those who behaved contrary to the teachings of the Church. Galileo was charged with committing just such a crime against the Church, but this was a crime associated with Galileo's beliefs concerning the _____ (4) sphere above—the sun and moon and planets. There were many doubts and suspicions about Galileo, but the _____ (5) charge against him was that he had promoted the Copernican theory that the sun—not the earth—was at the center of the universe. _____ (6), Galileo believed that the earth was moving around the sun. Pope Paul V himself had commanded Galileo to never support this *heliocentric* belief—that the sun is at the center. However, the later Pope Urban VIII felt it would be _____ (7) for Galileo to write about the two theories of *geocentrism* (earth at the center) and *heliocentrism* (sun at the center), so long as Galileo did not openly support heliocentrism. In his book on the *Two Chief World Systems*, Galileo did not _____ (8) declare his belief that the earth moved around the sun. However, one character in his book seemed to make the Pope himself look foolish. The Inquisition feared that Galileo's writing had the _____ (9) to lead people away from the Church, and so he was found guilty by the inquisitor and publication of any of Galileo's writing was forbidden. He spent the rest of his life under house arrest so that he would not be _____ (10) to the public.

E.   Write the letter of the word in each list that best completes the sentence.

1.   I'm not surprised that you thought these two photos were the same. The difference between them is nearly _____.

    a. *detect*
    b. *detected*

2.   Your last blood check _____ an increase in your white blood count, which could indicate an infection of some kind.

    c. *detection*
    d. *detective*

3.   When he was a kid, Matthew thought it would be so cool to be a _____ when he grew up, just like his TV heroes.

    e. *undetectable*

4.   Laura is afraid of dogs, because she feels their behavior is just too _____. She never knows what they will do next.

    f. *predict*
    g. *predictable*

5.   In some cultures, people believed they could _____ what will happen in the future using an animal's liver.

    h. *predicted*
    i. *prediction*

6.   Naijia became famous in Korea by offering people very accurate _____ of their futures.

    j. *unpredictable*

ASTRONOMY

Active reading can help you better understand a college text. Begin by discussing the questions below. Then carefully read the essay "Stars of the Ancients," taking notes on the main points and important details that you find in the text. Also select the best meaning for words highlighted in the right-hand column.

PREREADING DISCUSSION

1. What ancient civilizations have you studied? What can you tell about them and their beliefs and rituals?
2. How would ancient people interpret astronomical or celestial phenomena? What would they think about the stars and planets, the sun and the moon?
3. What do the sun and moon and stars mean to you? Is there any way that they can help us understand our lives? Or predict the future?

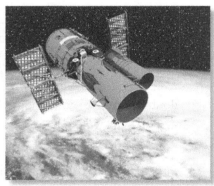

(1)   Can you remember what it was like when you were a child, staring up at those tiny lights in the night sky—before anyone ever explained it all to you, explained about planets and stars and galaxies? It is quite amazing how much we know now thanks to advances in scientific investigation,

5 assisted by modern telescopes that allow humans to detect light from very far away indeed. How far? You may have heard of light years, which refers to how far light can travel in one year. In one year, unobstructed light travels 5,865,696,000,000 miles. The *Hubble Space Telescope* was placed into low earth orbit back in 1990. It is capable of detecting near ultraviolet, visible, and

10 near infrared spectra of light, including light from remote stars that has traveled over immense distances. Hubble has detected light from stars that are over 10 billion light years away. This means that because of modern technology, humans can perceive light from stars that are 58,656,960,000,000,000,000,000 miles away! Most of us don't even know how to say a number that big![13]

15 (2)   Now try to imagine what it would be like interpreting all those lights without all that technology—no telescopes, only the naked human eye. You'd have no need for all of those big numbers, although you would be hard-pressed to explain what those tiny points of light were. And yet, that is precisely what humans have sought to do for millennia—explain the cosmos. Ancient

20 *Mesopotamia* (centered around modern day Iraq) was home to the first historical civilization on the planet. These were the first people anywhere to create a writing system—*cuneiform*—with which to record, well, everything—laws, stories, religious scriptures, and instructions on how to make a really good beer. Moreover, it was the *Babylonian* people of Mesopotamia who were the first to

25 write about the stars, recognizing that their movements were periodic and could be predicted through mathematical calculation.

(3)   However, more than that, Babylonian astronomers were the first to describe the planets. Without telescopes to assist them, they were observant enough to determine that some of those lights in the night sky looked and

30 behaved differently from all the rest. In particular, around the middle of the 17th century BC, astronomers in Babylon observed the planet *Venus* as she moved across the sky, recording her primary and last visible positions on the horizon before sunrise and after sunset. This is not to say that the Babylonians were purely interested in astronomical phenomena; their astronomy was primarily a

line 10: **remote**

a. distant
b. lonely
c. private

Another example:
A new tribe of natives has been discovered in a remote part of the Brazilian jungle.

A cuneiform inscription

114

35 means to astrological predictions. The same text that records the movements of
Venus also describes some 7,000 specific omens—signs of things that could
happen depending on where the celestial bodies happen to be at any moment.

(4)   The Babylonians identified five of the planets in our solar system:
Mercury, Venus, Mars, Saturn, and Jupiter. Furthermore, each planet was
40 associated with a particular Babylonian god, just as our modern names for the
planets in English derive from the names of Greek gods. *Jupiter*, for example,
was the great god *Marduk*, who had commanded King Hammurabi to write a
code of law for the people. *Venus* was *Ishtar*, goddess of love and fertility, as
well as of war. How these planets intersected and related with one another and
45 with other celestial bodies could warn people of good or bad things to come. The
timely rise of a new moon, for instance, might enable you to predict victory in
battle, or to foresee defeat if the moon rose prematurely.

(5)   Of course, these celestial bodies must have been visible in
the night sky to have played any role at all in the lives of the
50 ancients. Depending on where you are on the earth, some planets or
stars may always be visible or never visible, such as circumpolar
stars. Circumpolar stars are never seen to set or disappear below the
horizon, but seem instead simply to wander forever around one of
the celestial poles the entire night of every day of every year. This is
55 not to say that all polar stars seem to wander. In fact, one of the
most observed and indeed useful of stars in the polar sky seemed to
the ancients never to move at all. This was *Polaris*, the *Pole Star*, also
known as the *North Star*. Polaris has had many names over the
centuries since it was first noticed, but it's keen usefulness has been in
60 providing a fixed point in the sky for mariners to seek out, such as the Greeks
and Indians from at least the fifth century on. Identifying Polaris in the night sky
would help mariners to find their bearings in the open sea, much as later mariners
would use the compass to find true north.

Polaris, the North Star, with numerous
circumpolar stars seeming to spin around it

(6)   Polaris is not the only star to have attracted the attention of the ancients.
65 More often than not, the stars that have attracted the greatest attention have not
been the circumpolar stars, always visible in the sky, but those stars that rise and
set over the horizon, seeming to disappear and reappear as if on some grand
journey through the heavens. This is true of the brightest star in the night sky—
Sirius, a name that derives from the ancient Greeks. Sirius is also known as the
70 *Dog Star* because of its position in the constellation *Canis Major* ("Greater
Dog"). Its appearance in the night sky signaled the hot "dog days" of summer to
the ancient Greeks, whereas for Polynesians, it marked the beginning of winter.

(7)   Yet perhaps no one paid Sirius greater attention than did the ancient
Egyptians, who associated the Dog Star, also called *Sothis* (or *Sopdet* in
75 Egyptian) with the goddess *Isis*, who was the great Mother and goddess of magic.
For 70 days Sothis had been absent from the sky as Isis journeyed through the
underworld. The waters of the Nile valley fell and the land grew barren awaiting
Isis's return. Dwelling in the midst of a vast desert, the Egyptians depended on
the Nile River for their lives. However, the Nile valley in ancient times could
80 never have proven so fertile if not for the annual floods that covered the valley
with rain waters from far in the south. These flood waters brought fertile soil
from Sudan and deposited it in Egypt to the blessings of the Egyptian farmers.

---

line 35: means

a.   income
b.   definition
c.   method

Another example:
We need to find another
means of solving this
problem.

---

line 70: position

a.   location
b.   situation
c.   occupation

Another example:
The position of these
lights will not help the
audience to see the stage
better.

---

line 77: grew

a.   raised
b.   enlarged
c.   became

Another example:
After waiting in line for
two hours, I grew so tired
of this nonsense that I
went back home.

(8)   Such a great blessing was very welcome, as you can imagine, but it bore
the potential for political blessings as well. That is why it was so important for
85   the pharaohs of Egypt to be served by observant astronomers. When the king's
astronomer first saw Sothis in the eastern sky just before dawn, he informed the
pharaoh, who then appeared before the people declaring that he—the divine
king—would now cause the waters to rise and thereby bring fresh soil (and
consequently life) once again to the land of Egypt. No people love their king
90   quite so much as a happy, well-fed people.

Egyptian pharaoh Menkaura

(9)   Ancient Greeks, Romans, Egyptians, Babylonians—they all perceived
divinity and sacred power in the heavenly bodies and their actions in the night
sky. The ancient Indians were no exception to this. While Indian astronomy
dates back to at least 1500 BC, by the fourth century BC, Indian astronomers
95   were coming under the influence of the Greeks. However, prior to that,
astronomers in India had already identified some 27 constellations, 12 zodiacal
signs, and 7 planets, and not surprisingly all of this was intimately tied to Hindu
religious beliefs and practices. Texts such as the *Vedanga Jyotisa*, the oldest
Indian astronomical text, from around the 14th-12th centuries BC, were crucial for
100   determining and predicting the positions of stars, planets, and the moon.

(10)   However, the information provided by astronomers in India was also
used to determine the most auspicious time for marriage, making significant
decisions, and conducting *yajna* ("sacrifice"). Consequently, while one season of
the year may be viewed as favorable for weddings and celebrations, the
105   *Chaturma* season of some four holy months (around July to October) is
preferable for meditation, bathing in holy waters, and performing sacrifices.
These are typically not human or animal sacrifices, which would displease the
gods, but the burning of natural elements, such as clarified butter and milk, fruits
and vegetables, grains and flowers. Sacrifice has long been an essential means in
110   Vedic Hinduism[14] for liberating the self and allowing one to fully worship the
divine. By conducting the ritual of sacrifice at the appropriate time and with the
moon, let's say, in its proper place, humans can recognize and celebrate the very
order of the universe established by divinity.

A worshipful Hindu monk

(11)   The Chinese developed a *lunisolar calendar*. Likewise, the Hindus
115   created a calendar based on a solar year (around 365 days) but composed of lunar
months (months of approximately 27–28 days each based on the cycles of the
moon). Also like the Hindu Indians, the Chinese perceived a system of
constellations based on the movements of the moon rather than on the position of
the sun. The Chinese referred to these constellations as *mansions*, of which there
120   are 28, divided into four celestial regions of stars. They divided stars into these
four regions based on the position of each star relative to Polaris, the North Star.

(12)   Chinese astronomy was not tied exclusively to religious beliefs or
mythologies. Rather, astronomers could better tell time as they observed the
progress of the moon along its path through each of these 28 mansions, such as
125   the Heart in the East and the Girl in the North, the Stomach of the West and the
Ghost of the South. Over the centuries, the Chinese continued to expand on their
understanding of the heavens, illustrating elaborate star maps and recording some
1,600 solar and lunar eclipses. The sun and the moon mattered as much to
Chinese astronomers as did the stars. Chinese mathematician *Jing Fang* (78–37
130   BC) echoed Aristotle's observation that the light of the moon is in fact reflected
light that originates from the sun.

line 128: matter
a.   *topic*
b.   *be important*
c.   *substance*
Another example:
Doctors say that it matters how much sleep you get each night.

ASTRONOMY

A. **Which of the following statements best expresses the thesis or main idea of the essay "Stars of the Ancients"? Circle the number of the correct answer.**

1. Various ancient cultures pursued detailed studies of the heavens, often in order to understand and predict the will of supernatural beings.

2. Without modern devices to assist them, ancient cultures pursued imprecise beliefs about the lights they saw in the night sky.

3. Astronomy can assist humans in many ways, such as in understanding past cultures, predicting seasonal events, and even navigating around the world.

B. **Several cultures are mentioned in this text, all with a tradition of astronomical observations and research. Write the appropriate letters of the cultures below to indicate which cultures were associated with each interest or accomplishment described in the essay. More than one answer may be possible.**

> **(a)** Greek   **(b)** Egyptian   **(c)** Babylonian   **(d)** Indian   **(e)** Chinese

1. _____ The first culture to write about the stars.

2. _____ Used astronomical observations for religious or spiritual purposes.

3. _____ Associated the Dog Star with floods.

4. _____ Recorded their observations of Polaris, the North Star.

5. _____ Associated individual planets with specific gods.

6. _____ Argued that light from the sun reflected over the moon.

7. _____ Developed a lunisolar calendar.

8. _____ Observed the moon passing through 28 mansions.

9. _____ The first culture to predict the movement of the stars using mathematical calculations.

10. _____ Identified various constellations of stars.

11. _____ Astronomers helped the king to demonstrate his great powers.

12. _____ Used their observations of celestial bodies to choose the most appropriate times for performing sacrifices.

13. _____ Identified seven planets.

14. _____ Recorded some 7,000 omens related to the positions of celestial bodies.

15. _____ The first culture to record their observations of planets.

16. _____ Recorded their observations of the Dog Star, Sirius.

17. _____ Recorded some 1,600 solar and lunar eclipses.

18. _____ Used astronomy to celebrate the divine order in the universe.

C. *Each of the sentences below from the essay "Stars of the Ancients" includes at least one word that usually refers to something else, such as a pronoun or relative pronoun. Remember though that sometimes the pronoun "it" does not really refer to anything. Instead, it functions as a subject in a sentence that otherwise has no subject, such as in the sentence "It is hot outside." This is the "dummy IT" that does not refer to anything. Circle what each of the underlined reference words refers to in these sentences. If the pronoun below is a "dummy IT," then do not circle anything.*

1. <u>It</u> is quite amazing how much we know now thanks to advances in scientific investigation, assisted by modern telescopes <u>that</u> allow humans to detect light from very far away indeed. *(lines 3–6)*

2. The *Hubble Space Telescope* was placed into low earth orbit back in 1990. <u>It</u> is capable of detecting near ultraviolet, visible, and near infrared spectra of light, including light from remote stars <u>that</u> has traveled over immense distances. *(lines 8–11)*

3. And yet, <u>that</u> is precisely what humans have sought to do for millennia—explain the cosmos. *(lines 18–19)*

4. Ancient *Mesopotamia* (centered around modern day Iraq) was home to the first historical civilization on the planet. <u>These</u> were the first people anywhere to create a writing system—*cuneiform*—with <u>which</u> to record, well, everything. *(lines 19–22)*

5. How these planets intersected and related with <u>one another</u> and with other celestial bodies could warn people of good or bad things to come. *(lines 44–45)*

6. Polaris has had many names over the centuries since <u>it</u> was first noticed, but <u>it's</u> keen usefulness has been in providing a fixed point in the sky for mariners to seek out. *(lines 58–60)*

7. Yet perhaps no one paid Sirius greater attention than did the ancient Egyptians, <u>who</u> associated the Dog Star, also called *Sothis* (or *Sopdet* in Egyptian) with the goddess *Isis*, <u>who</u> was the great Mother and goddess of magic. *(lines 73–75)*

8. Such a great blessing was very welcome, as you can imagine, but <u>it</u> bore the potential for political blessings as well. That is why <u>it</u> was so important for the pharaohs of Egypt to be served by observant astronomers. *(lines 83–85)*

9. Ancient Greeks, Romans, Egyptians, Babylonians—<u>they</u> all perceived divinity and sacred power in the heavenly bodies and <u>their</u> actions in the night sky. *(lines 91–93)*

10. The Chinese referred to these constellations as *mansions*, of <u>which</u> there are 28, divided into four celestial regions of stars. *(lines 119–20)*

ASTRONOMY

A. PURPOSES AND TYPES OF TRANSITION WORDS

The more information that we communicate to others, the more necessary it becomes to clearly indicate how bits of information are related to one another. Does one idea contrast with another? Is it an example or cause of something else? Are we seeking to express additional information on the same topic? Did one event happen before or after another? Or at the same time? Look at the following sentences. What is the purpose of the underlined transition words?

1. Mary really liked the movie. <u>However</u>, Martha hated it!

       a. comparing things   *b. contrasting things*   *c. giving examples*

2. Why don't you work on your essay <u>while</u> I get dinner ready.

       a. emphasizing an idea   *b. time & sequencing*   *c. additional information*

3. <u>I feel</u> this class is just too difficult for me right now with all the work I have to do.

       a. cause & effect   *b. expressing an opinion*   *c. contrasting things*

B. For every kind of relationship that ideas can have, there are appropriate transition words to use—words that show how these ideas are related to one another. You likely know many of these transition words already. Here are a number of examples of transition words. Can you write them under the correct category of transitions?

after	*for example*	*eventually*	*such as*	*in addition*
moreover	*due to*	*surely*	*similarly*	*thus*
while	*correspondingly*	*for instance*	*initially*	*in fact*
likewise	*furthermore*	*because of*	*it seems to me*	*on the other hand*
consequently	*although*	*in my view*	*besides*	*whereas*
I believe	*certainly*	*in common*	*however*	*indeed*

Types of Transitions			
additional information	**cause & effect**	**comparing things**	**contrasting things**
emphasizing an idea	**expressing an opinion**	**giving examples**	**time & sequencing**

C. **Look at the following sentences from our reading. First, <u>underline</u> the transition word you find in each sentence. Then, circle the letter (a, b, or c) of the transition word or phrase that is closest in meaning to the transition word that you have underlined.**

1. It is quite amazing how much we know now thanks to advances in scientific investigation. *(lines 3–4)*

    a. *moreover*   b. *for example*   c. *because of*

2. You'd have no need for all of those big numbers, although you would be hard-pressed to explain what those tiny points of light were. *(lines 16–18)*

    a. *even though*   b. *meanwhile*   c. *so*

3. Moreover, it was the Babylonian people of Mesopotamia who were the first to write about the stars. *(lines 24–25)*

    a. *furthermore*   b. *before*   c. *and*

4. However, more than that, Babylonian astronomers were the first to describe the planets. *(lines 27–28)*

    a. *if*   b. *thereafter*   c. *but*

5. The Babylonians identified five of the planets in our solar system: Mercury, Venus, Mars, Saturn, and Jupiter. Furthermore, each planet was associated with a particular Babylonian god. *(lines 38–40)*

    a. *on the other hand*   b. *besides*   c. *thus*

6. Depending where you are on the earth, some planets or stars may always be visible or never visible, such as circumpolar stars. *(lines 50–52)*

    a. *surely*   b. *likewise*   c. *for instance*

7. In fact, one of the most observed and indeed useful of stars in the polar sky seemed to the ancients never to move at all. *(lines 55–57)*

    a. *I believe*   b. *indeed*   c. *initially*

8. Its appearance in the night sky signaled the hot "dog days" of summer to the ancient Greeks, whereas for Polynesians, it marked the beginning of winter. *(lines 71–72)*

    a. *due to*   b. *eventually*   c. *in contrast*

9. Consequently, while one season of the year may be viewed as favorable for weddings and celebrations, the *Chaturma* season of some four holy months (around July to October) is preferable for meditation. *(lines 103–06)*

    a. *certainly*   b. *thus*   c. *although*

10. The Chinese developed a *lunisolar calendar*. Likewise, the Hindus created a calendar based on a solar year (around 365 days) but composed of lunar months. *(lines 114–16)*

    a. *similarly*   b. *in fact*   c. *such as*

11. Astronomers could better tell time as they observed the progress of the moon along its path through each of these 28 mansions, such as the Heart in the East and the Girl in the North. *(lines 123–25)*

    a. *for example*   b. *in common*   c. *similarly*

12. *Complete the following text by circling the most appropriate transition words.*

I remember so well the first time I saw the night sky outside of the city. When you live in an urban center, you don't really see the sky **(1)** *because of / however / indeed* all the city lights. As a kid, **(2)** *it seemed to me / furthermore / due to* that there were only a few dozen stars in the sky at night. **(3)** *Likewise / Besides / Consequently*, when my father first told me about the Milky Way with its billions of stars, I really did not believe him. **(4)** *After / Similarly / Whereas*, I did not believe his descriptions of the constellations. I had no idea what he was talking about when he said that there were animals and heroes and objects in the sky at night, **(5)** *such as / thus / in fact* a bear or an archer or a beautiful queen. I certainly did not see them. **(6)** *Correspondingly / In my view / On the other hand*, the sky was nothing but a graying darkness with a few faint points of light flickering here and there.

(7) *Eventually / Furthermore / I believe*, the time came when my father said that I really needed to see it all for myself—what he called the "real sky." **(8)** *Moreover / Initially / Thus*, one Friday morning he said, "Pack your bag. **(9)** *After / Because of / In addition* school, we are driving up to Lake Alpine in the mountains." He picked me up from school that day, and we drove and drove far away from the city. That evening we reached the campground and unloaded the car. **(10)** *Thus / While / In common* Papa was setting up the camp, I wandered around and thought about how quiet it was up there. **(11)** *Initially / Besides / However*, I was a little scared, to be honest. I mean, it was pretty dark after the sun set, darker than any place in the city. **(12)** *In my view / Surely / In contrast*, there were animals in the trees and scurrying across the ground, and they made these sounds—sounds that were small, but which made me jump sometimes.

When the tent was set up and everything ready, my father grabbed his flashlight and led me through the trees and away from the camp. I walked beside him, keeping my eyes on the light bouncing across the ground and avoiding the obstacles in our path, **(13)** *for instance / due to / likewise* a big rock here or a fallen tree branch there. Or animals. **(14)** *Indeed / Besides / Although* I had not ever seen a real snake, I was sure there were snakes hiding along the path, waiting to bite me. **(15)** *In fact / For example / Similarly*, I was staring so intently at the ground that I had no idea what was above me, not until my father stopped walking and said, "Look up." I could not believe my eyes! **(16)** *Although / Certainly / Eventually* there could never be so many stars in the sky as I saw that night. Where had they all been hiding? **(17)** *On the other hand / I believe / Correspondingly* that was the moment—the exact moment—when I knew what I wanted to do with my life. Today I am an astronomer **(18)** *due to / furthermore / while* my father and the night he showed me the real sky.

ASTRONOMY   JOURNAL WRITING 6.1

Choose from the following options for your journal writing assignment:

1. The essay "Stars of the Ancients" summarizes perspectives of ancient people concerning the cosmos, including the views of ancient Babylonians, Egyptians, Greeks, Indians, and Chinese. Of course, the information we have read is very brief. Astronomers and researchers in each of these cultures have gathered far more information about the stars and other celestial bodies. Use whatever resources are available to you—your classmates, a library, the Internet—to expand your understanding of how any ancient culture around the world has viewed the heavens. Write about what you have learned about at least one ancient culture and their knowledge of astronomical phenomena.

2. Imagine that you now live long ago, a member of an ancient culture prior to the acquisition of astronomical knowledge. In essence, you are the first astronomer of your culture—a pioneer in the study of the heavens. How would you interpret the things you see in the sky above? Do you think you would have understood the lights in the sky to be stars, like our own sun? Or would you have perceived them to be something else? Gods perhaps or spirits? Alien beings or holes in space? It is your job to write a description of the heavens—of the stars, the sun, the moon—and what you write will be used to teach the next generation of children in your culture what they should know about the heavens.

3. As we have read, ancient people often used astronomical observations to enhance their understanding of religion or spirituality, or to predict events in their own lives. In many different cultures, astrology is practiced as a means of predicting human events based on a belief that celestial phenomena interact with or affect people on earth. What do you think about this belief? Has it ever been of importance to you? Are you familiar with your astrological sign? With your horoscope? Describe the value of astrology in your home culture or in your own personal life. What does all of that mean to you?

4. The ancient Chinese perceived constellations among clusters of stars and classified them into 28 mansions, representing such concepts as the Heart in the East, the Girl in the North, the Stomach of the West, and the Ghost of the South. Western constellations are often tied to classical Greek or Roman mythology. The constellation of Cassiopeia is named for a queen of great vanity who boasted that she and her daughter were more beautiful than sea nymphs. Her boasting incited the God of the Sea, Poseidon, to punish Cassiopeia. She was bound to a chair in the heavens to forever spin around the night sky. Are you familiar with any constellations? Write the names of several constellations (from any system of constellations in the world) and describe what these constellations are believed to represent.

The constellation of Cassiopeia

ASTRONOMY   VOCABULARY 6.2

A. Here are our target vocabulary for Reading 2 in this unit:

accelerate	generate	period	resolution
approximately	hypothesis	rational	revolution
controversial	impose	relevant	velocity

B. You know that one word can have a variety of meanings in English. Write the letter of the synonym that best expresses the meaning of the vocabulary word in each sentence below.

1. _____ There was a **period** in my life when I thought I would never find the right person for me.

2. _____ What class are you taking first **period**? I'm taking the Introduction to Biology class.

3. _____ A girl could get her first **period** fairly early—maybe age 8—or later, around age 12 or 13.

a. term
b. hour
c. phase
d. measure
e. cycle

---

4. _____ I wish this screen had better **resolution**. I cannot see any of the details in this image.

5. _____ The **resolution** of this court is that the defendant pay a $1,000 fine and perform 100 hours of community service.

6. _____ I thought he would quit school after his poor grade on the first test, but his **resolution** keeps him going and going.

f. decision
g. verdict
h. determination
i. courage
j. visual quality

C. For each of the following vocabulary words, there are two antonyms and one synonym. Circle the synonym.

1.	**accelerate**	decelerate	slow down	speed up
2.	**approximately**	around	exactly	precisely
3.	**controversial**	undisputed	contentious	unarguable
4.	**hypothesis**	fact	theory	truth
5.	**impose**	prevent	oblige	neglect
6.	**rational**	irrational	illogical	reasonable
7.	**relevant**	pertinent	irrelevant	insignificant

D. *Complete the following text by circling the correct form of each word.*

Today there are **(1)** *approximate / approximately / approximation* seven billion people in the world. That's quite a large number. And the birth rate, at least in some parts of the world, keeps **(2)** *accelerate / acceleration / accelerating.* Am I the only one who is worried about this? I am sure this is a **(3)** *controverter / controversial / controversy* point of view, but I really think the human race needs to stop having so many babies. This is the only world we have, and I do not believe the resources of this world will be enough for everyone. Especially when each **(4)** *generate / generating / generation* thinks that it can still have it all and have lots of children, too. I would **(5)** *hypothesis / hypothetical / hypothesize* that big trouble is coming in two decades. I can easily imagine many **(6)** *revolutionary / revolutions / revolting* beginning around the world, especially when there is not enough food or water to feed everyone. Of course, I could be wrong; maybe I am just not **(7)** *rational / rationalize / rationally* enough about this problem. Maybe the scale of this problem is just not as **(8)** *impose / imposing / imposition* as I imagine it to be. But I kind of doubt it.

E. *Each of these sentences includes one of our vocabulary words. In the space provided, write the final suffix from the highlighted vocabulary word and then check what part of speech that suffix creates. Then write three more English words that have the same suffix as the highlighted word.*

1. There are **approximately** 50,000 students at this college.

    suffix _____ ☐ *noun*   ☐ *verb*   ☐ *adjective*   ☐ *adverb*

    a. _____   *b.* _____   *c.* _____

2. Abortion was already a **controversial** issue when I was a kid and it still is today.

    suffix _____ ☐ *noun*   ☐ *verb*   ☐ *adjective*   ☐ *adverb*

    a. _____   *b.* _____   *c.* _____

3. The new law will **generate** the kind of support that this government really needs right now.

    suffix _____ ☐ *noun*   ☐ *verb*   ☐ *adjective*   ☐ *adverb*

    a. _____   *b.* _____   *c.* _____

4. Your argument is interesting, yes, but it is not at all **relevant** to the problem we are discussing.

    suffix _____ ☐ *noun*   ☐ *verb*   ☐ *adjective*   ☐ *adverb*

    a. _____   *b.* _____   *c.* _____

5. If you have a strong **resolution** to succeed in school, I am sure that you will succeed.

    suffix _____ ☐ *noun*   ☐ *verb*   ☐ *adjective*   ☐ *adverb*

    a. _____   *b.* _____   *c.* _____

ASTRONOMY

Before you read the following essay, discuss with your peers the people and concepts listed below. Then carefully read the essay "An Astronomical Revolution," taking notes on the main points and important details that you find in the text. Also select the best meaning for words highlighted in the right-hand column.

PREREADING DISCUSSION

In the following essay, you will read about a number of important figures in a period of astronomical research when major changes were happening. Share with your peers what you know about the following people and concepts:

1. Galileo Galilei   **2.** Isaac Newton   **3.** Johannes Kepler   **4.** Nicolaus Copernicus
5. geocentrism   **6.** heliocentrism   **7.** gravity   **8.** orbit

(1)   The more time that ancient astronomers spent studying the heavens, the more obvious it became to them that most things they saw in the night sky were actually moving. As their understanding of the heavens grew, they became convinced that most of the stars and all of the observable planets were not fixed
5   in a single location, but changed their location according to a peculiar *orbit*. In most cases, their hypothesis was that these orbits were circular and that each celestial object, including the sun and the moon as well, traveled in a circle around a central point. The relevant question became, what was that central point around which the heavens revolved?

10   (2)   If you had posed this question to the greatest minds of the ancient world, most (but not all) researchers would have agreed—the earth is the center of the universe. *Aristotle* (384–322 BC) himself supported this *geocentric* view—the principle that the earth is at the center and that all other observable bodies in the heavens travel around the earth. In this model of the universe, the earth is
15   unmoving—a fixed point in space. Of course we know the earth does not move, because if it were moving or spinning, we would feel it move, right? In fact, if the earth were spinning—as *Ptolemy* (c.90–168) argued—terrible winds would arise and we would fly off the earth into space.[15] As time passed, one would expect centuries of research and observation to demand a new answer to our
20   question. What seems to have delayed this demand was that for a millennium or so researchers continued to accept the same faulty belief in *geocentrism* promoted by Aristotle and other ancient or classical writers.

(3)   This geocentric view was even supported by rational thinkers in all three Abrahamic faiths: Judaism, Christianity, and Islam. *Galileo Galilei* (1564–1642)
25   was brought before the Inquisition in 1633 to answer charges against him of heresy because he seemed to support the extremely controversial notion of *heliocentrism*—that the earth was moving around the sun. The Pope of the Catholic Church and the inquisitors could not allow such a sin to go unpunished. It was the belief of the leaders of the Catholic Church—and therefore the
30   obligatory belief of all Catholic Christians—that the sun orbited around the earth, and they imposed this belief on others. Galileo was compelled to agree with the Pope, but just to make sure, the inquisitors commanded that Galileo's writings be destroyed, that he not be allowed to publish anything again, and eventually he was moved to house arrest for the remainder of his days on earth.

line 10: pose

a. present
b. pretend
c. stand

Another example:
Your question poses a problem for us unless we can find a solution quickly.

line 15: fixed

a. repaired
b. attached
c. unmoving

Another example:
From his fixed position atop the hill, he could see clearly in all directions.

Galileo Galilei.

35   (4)   The man who had most influenced Galileo to adopt a heliocentric view was the Polish mathematician and astronomer *Nicolaus Copernicus* (1473–1543). Copernicus noted earlier heliocentric views—expressed in classical Greece, for example, by *Aristarchus* (c.310–230 BC)—but he was still reluctant to publish his own heliocentric model, which put the sun at the center of the universe. Like

40   Charles Darwin centuries later, Copernicus feared the negative reaction his observations would evoke in people. Considering what would happen to Galileo some years later, you can imagine why Copernicus lacked the resolution to move forward and publish. In the event, Copernicus died even as his theory was finally coming into print, and he was spared the inevitable backlash.

Nikolaus Kopernikus.

45   (5)   The heliocentric model of Copernicus solved two issues that had plagued geocentric thinkers for years: 1) why the other planets in the night sky seemed to grow brighter and then duller over time and 2) why those planets sometimes seemed to move forward and then back again, a phenomenon referred to as *retrograde motion*. If the earth were unmoving and everything else moved in

50   tight circular orbits around the earth, there should be neither retrograde motion nor varying brightness in the other planets. Mars, for example, would always be the same distance from the earth, would always seem to be moving forward, and would always appear to reflect the same amount of light.

line 45: model

a.   *a worthy example*
b.   *a painter's subject*
c.   *a representation*

Another example:
Freud's model of the mind included three levels of consciousness.

(6)   However, if the earth too were moving in its own orbit around the sun,

55   then sometimes it would be closer to Mars and sometimes further away because of their different orbits. Due to the fact that the earth is closer to the sun than is Mars, the earth orbits the sun faster than does Mars. When the earth is closer to Mars, Mars appears brighter. When it is further away, Mars appears duller. And when the earth, with its swifter orbit, passes the slower moving Mars, it seems

60   that Mars, in relation to distant fixed stars, is going backwards for a time before once again moving forward. Copernicus still falsely believed, like Galileo, that all orbits were perfectly circular. Moreover, his mathematical model for predicting the positions of the other planets was far from correct. Nonetheless, his model did at least explain away these two tricky points.

65   (7)   One problem with the theories of Copernicus was finally solved by another prominent figure in the field of astronomy, *Johannes Kepler* (1571–1630). It was the work of Kepler, a German mathematician and astronomer, that laid the groundwork for the theory of *universal gravitation*[16] proposed by Isaac Newton in the late 1600s. Kepler was very enthusiastic about the work of

70   Copernicus, but he pursued his own astronomical research with a view to harmonizing faith and science. He strongly disagreed that the observations of astronomers, including the heliocentric model, contradicted the Bible. Instead, he suggested a religious approach to understanding the heavens. Of course the sun is in the center of all things, just as God is the center of all things. The sun

75   represents God, the sphere of stars around us represents Jesus, and the space between the sun and the stars is the Holy Ghost.

Johannes Kepler.

(8)   However, Kepler is perhaps best known for having corrected a significant failing in the model generated by Copernicus—circular orbits. Through careful observation, and the application of his own mathematical model,

80   Kepler determined three laws that describe the motions of the planets. According to his *First Law*, planets do not actually move around the sun in circles. Rather, planetary orbit is *elliptical*, like a slightly flattened circle. Moreover, this ellipsis does not have the sun at its center. Instead, Kepler identified two focal points

85 along the major axis of the ellipsis—one focus to the left of center and one to the right. The sun occupies one focus point in the elliptical orbit of a planet, while the other focus is occupied by, well, empty space equidistant from the center of the ellipsis, but on the other side.

(9)   Kepler was correct about elliptical orbits, but the very fact of an elliptical rather than a circular orbit, with the sun off-center within
90 the ellipsis, meant that at any given time traveling along its orbit, a planet moves closer or further away from the sun. This led to Kepler's *Second Law* of planetary motion, namely that as a planet approaches its nearest position to the sun at one end of the elliptical orbit—known as the *perihelion*—its speed of movement increases.
95 The closer a planet moves to a position furthest from the sun—known as its *aphelion*—essentially moving away from the sun, the velocity of the planet decreases.

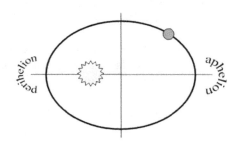

(10)   Kepler's *Third Law* suggests that the *orbital period* of any planet—the number of earth days or years required by that planet to complete one orbit
100 around the sun—varies in direct relation to the radius of its orbit. The smaller the radius, the shorter the orbital period. This makes perfect sense in light of Kepler's Second Law, which noted how planets accelerate when they draw closer to the sun. The nearest planet to the sun is Mercury, and it takes Mercury approximately 88 days to orbit the sun. The earth takes around 365 days to
105 complete its orbit. Neptune, the furthest planet from the sun (and the planet with the largest radius in its elliptical orbit) takes nearly 165 years to complete a single orbit of the sun. While we may celebrate each of our birthdays based on one complete orbital period of the earth, any given human being will be born, live, and die before Neptune completes even a single orbit.

110 (11)   While Kepler's laws were more or less correct when applied to planetary motion, nobody—including Kepler—could actually explain why they were correct. Nor did Kepler seek to apply his three laws to any celestial objects other than the planets. For this next step in understanding the motion of objects in the sky, a truly towering figure in this astronomical revolution was needed, and that
115 man was *Isaac Newton* (1642–1727). Newton was a remarkable man, a pioneer in physics and astronomy, the man who constructed a new understanding of color by examining how white light is broken down into the many colors of the spectrum when it passes through a prism. He further invented the first practical reflecting telescope, essential in astronomical observations, which uses mirrors to
120 reflect light from a distant object in order to create an image of that object.

(12)   Newton expanded on the work of Kepler concerning planetary motion, and of Galileo, who first described how force causes motion, and how motion can be understood in terms of velocity, which Galileo measured according to speed and direction. Newton observed, as Galileo had, that an object at rest—
125 say, an apple hanging from a tree—only accelerates because of a force. That force is gravity. The mass of the earth that we live on exerts a gravitational pull on all of us. The hanging apple is being drawn to the earth by this gravity. Should its stem, which holds it to the branch of the tree, break, then the force of gravity will pull the apple to the earth. Likewise, Newton argued, the orbit of the
130 planets described by Kepler are caused by the same gravitational force. The earth is constantly falling towards the sun, drawn by the force of the sun's gravitational pull, but because the sun moves as well, the earth never reaches it.

Isaak Newton.

> **line 98: law**
>
> a. religious covenant
> b. physical principle
> c. government rule
>
> **Another example:**
> *Hubble's law describes the change in wave lengths of light as objects in deep space move away from the earth.*

> **line 127: drawn**
>
> a. illustrated
> b. pulled
> c. tense
>
> **Another example:**
> *Before the automobile, people relied on horse-drawn wagons for their transportation.*

ASTRONOMY

A. *Which of the following statements best expresses the thesis or main idea of the essay "Astronomical Revolution"? Circle the number of the correct answer.*

1. The research of astronomers throughout history has been opposed by religious movements—such as Judaism, Christianity, and Islam—which seek to maintain the truth according to scripture even when evidence contradicts their beliefs.

2. Great advances in astronomical and mathematical research—led by men like Galileo, Kepler, Copernicus, and Newton—have brought us closer to understanding how the universe is organized and how planets move.

3. While men like Kepler, Galileo, and Copernicus offered important insights into astronomy, Newton revolutionized astronomical research and our understanding of the universe by taking the research of these earlier figures a step further.

B. *Skim through the essay once again and write the name of the researcher(s) associated with the following beliefs, actions, or discoveries in Astronomy. There may be more than one answer.*

    (a) Aristotle   (b) Ptolemy   (c) Galileo   (d) Copernicus (e) Kepler   (f) Newton

1. _____ Was charged with heresy by the Inquisition.

2. _____ The sun revolves around the earth.

3. _____ Planetary orbits are circular.

4. _____ Explained how the planets seem to grow brighter and duller as they move.

5. _____ If the earth were moving, we would fly off into space.

6. _____ Invented the first practical reflecting telescope.

7. _____ Recognized that planets further from the sun take longer to complete an orbit.

8. _____ Deeply influenced the ideas of Galileo.

9. _____ Was placed under house arrest.

10. _____ The earth revolves around the sun.

11. _____ Offered an explanation for the retrograde motion of planets.

12. _____ Observed that an object at rest only accelerates because of a force.

13. _____ Tried to find harmony between religion and science in astronomy.

14. _____ Planetary orbits are elliptical.

15. _____ Used a prism to break down white light into the colors of the spectrum.

16. _____ Identified the perihelion and aphelion of planetary orbits.

17. _____ Gravitational force also affects planetary orbits.

18. _____ The earth is an unmoving fixed point in space.

C. *Academic essays are typically written in an order and follow a pattern of organization that allows the reader to understand more easily what the writer is saying: to learn the information the writer has shared or to follow the argument that the writer has made. A logical order in your own writing should make your compositions clearer and more effective. Below are fifteen main ideas. Twelve of these main ideas match the twelve paragraphs of the essay "Astronomical Revolution." Write the number of the paragraph next to the appropriate main idea. Write an "X" next to the three remaining main ideas.*

    a. _____ Kepler disagreed with Copernicus about circular orbits, instead promoting his law of elliptical orbits for the planets.

    b. _____ Ancient observers, such as Aristotle and Ptolemy, argued that all celestial objects revolve around the earth.

    c. _____ Kepler argued that the velocity of a planet in motion varies as it approaches its orbital perihelion and aphelion.

    d. _____ Isaac Newton was a remarkable inventor and observer who helped us to better understand where the colors of the spectrum come from.

    e. _____ Despite his reluctance to do so, Copernicus finally published his heliocentric model of planetary motion.

    f. _____ The heliocentric model of Copernicus helped to explain why planets seem to change in luminosity and move sometimes back, sometimes forward in their orbits.

    g. _____ The observations of ancient astronomers led to the belief that all objects in the sky orbit around a central point.

    h. _____ A planet like Mars seems sometimes brighter or duller because it is not always the same distance from the earth, while its slower orbit makes it seem to go back and forth.

    i. _____ Copernicus learned from the ancient astronomer Aristarchus about how the sun, not the earth, was in the center of our planetary system.

    j. _____ Kepler sought to advance our knowledge of the universe while also striving for harmony between science and faith.

    k. _____ Galileo Galilei was charged with heresy by the Inquisition for supporting the heliocentric model of the planets.

    l. _____ Kepler's final law concerned how the radius of an orbit can be tied to the number of days it takes for a planet to complete its orbit.

    m. _____ Newton expanded on Galileo's argument about force causing acceleration by identifying that gravity was the force that led to planetary motion.

    n. _____ Galileo was challenged by the Catholic Pope and eventually faced house arrest until the day he died.

    o. _____ Nobody could explain why Kepler's laws of planetary motion were correct until Isaac Newton studied the problem.

ASTRONOMY

A. REVIEWING SUBJECT-VERB AGREEMENT

Subject-verb agreement is one of those rules that we learn quite early on. Even the simplest of English sentences requires us to pay attention to this rule and to make sure that the SUBJECT of the sentence and the VERB are in agreement. What do we mean by "in agreement"? Look at the subjects and verbs in these sentences. Can you explain what is wrong with two of the sentences?

1. *My friend is a student at this college.*

2. *His Math teacher come from India.*

3. *The class are very difficult.*

4. *However, he always gets good grades on his assignments.*

We also learn how to distinguish between countable and uncountable nouns, and how uncountable nouns are therefore treated as singular nouns that agree with the third-person singular verb form, even when the noun we use seems to describe many different parts or elements.

5. *We have collected data over the last six months, and this <u>data</u> <u>describes</u> an intriguing change in how people use their computers.*

6. *I usually enjoy dinner at this restaurant, but tonight the <u>rice</u> <u>is</u> cold.*

7. *The <u>traffic</u> this morning <u>was</u> terrible. Did you see all those cars on the road?*

8. *The inspector found a lot of evidence, but this <u>evidence</u> <u>does not prove</u> that I am guilty.*

Nonetheless, one of the most persistent grammatical mistakes students make involves subject-verb agreement. There is a good reason for this. As a college student reading academic texts, you are expected to understand sentences that are far more complex than the examples we have just seen above. So long as the verb comes immediately after the subject, you can more easily recognize whether or not the subject and verb agree with one another. However, if more information comes between the subject and verb, it can be harder to follow the rules of subject-verb agreement. For example, look at these sentences. Underline the main subject and circle the main verb.

9. *As the years have passed, many people in our society, without even knowing they do so, have come to rely upon anonymous sources of information.*

10. *Our best student, who is just one of many students struggling to complete a graduate program of study in one of the top universities in the country, works a full-time job.*

11. *Perhaps the most important decision that any man or woman can make obliges us to consider the consequences and responsibilities of raising a family.*

12. *Continued smoking by so many young people around the world demonstrates how quickly humans forget the lessons they had supposedly learned about the causes of cancer.*

13. *What may surprise you most about Gordon McCandless's new novel is that such a famous mystery writer has chosen to write a romance novel this time around.*

B. **The last three examples above illustrate certain grammatical constructions that may make it harder for you to match the main subject with the main verb.**

1. Perhaps <u>the most important decision</u> <u>that any man or woman can make</u> obliges us to consider the
   SUBJECT   SUBJECT RELATIVE CLAUSE   VERB
consequences and responsibilities of raising a family.

2. <u>Continued smoking</u> <u>by so many young people around the world</u> <u>demonstrates</u> how quickly
   SUBJECT   PREPOSITIONAL PHRASE   VERB
humans forget the lessons they had supposedly learned about the causes of cancer.

3. <u>What may surprise you most about Gordon McCandless's new novel</u> <u>is</u> that such a famous
            NOUN CLAUSE   VERB
mystery writer has chosen to write a romance novel this time around.

Be careful with these constructions. If you are uncertain about subject-verb agreement in your own sentences, go back over your sentence again and identify the main subject and verb to ensure that they are in agreement.

C. **Look at these sentences from our reading. In each sentence, underline the subject and circle the verb. Some sentences have more than one subject-verb combination. Number the subjects and verbs to identify which verb goes with which subject.**

1. As their understanding of the heavens grew, they became convinced that most of the stars and all of the observable planets were not fixed in a single location, but changed their location according to a peculiar orbit. *(lines 3–5)*

2. What seems to have delayed this demand was that for a millennium or so researchers continued to accept the same faulty belief in *geocentrism* promoted by Aristotle and other ancient or classical writers. *(lines 20–22)*

3. The man who had most influenced Galileo to adopt a heliocentric view was the Polish mathematician and astronomer *Nicolaus Copernicus* (1473–1543). *(lines 35–36)*

4. The sun represents God, the sphere of stars around us represents Jesus, and the space between the sun and the stars is the Holy Ghost. *(lines 74–76)*

5. Through careful observation, and the application of his own mathematical model, Kepler determined three laws that describe the motions of the planets. *(lines 79–80)*

6. Kepler was correct about elliptical orbits, but the very fact of an elliptical rather than a circular orbit, with the sun off-center within the ellipsis, meant that at any given time traveling along its orbit, a planet moves closer or further away from the sun. *(lines 88–91)*

7. Kepler's Third Law suggests that the *orbital period* of any planet—the number of earth days or years required by that planet to complete one orbit around the sun—varies in direction relation to the radius of its orbit. *(lines 98–100)*

8. The mass of the earth that we live on exerts a gravitational pull on all of us. *(lines 126–27)*

D. **Another factor that might cause some misunderstanding over subject-verb agreement is linked to the use of quantifiers, such as "most" or "many" or "every." Quantifiers tend to make us think of plurals. However, a subject with a quantifier must still be seen as either countable or uncountable, and that will affect subject-verb agreement. For example, "homework" is not countable, but "student" is countable.**

> *Most homework is due on Monday after the weekend.*

> *Most students are not very happy to spend the weekend doing homework.*

There are clues that can help you to understand the difference. Some quantifiers are only used with countable nouns or with uncountable nouns:

> **COUNTABLE NOUNS:**   *few, a few, several, many, a large number*
> **UNCOUNTABLE NOUNS:**   *little, a little, much, a great deal, a large amount*

E. **In each of these sentences, circle the correct form of the verb. Pay attention to things that separate nouns and subjects, such as noun clauses, prepositional phrases, and subject relative clauses. Also, be careful of countable and uncountable nouns and quantifiers.**

1. A great deal of time *is / are* spent worrying about what classes to text next. You should focus on the classes you are taking now.

2. Writing two 10-page essays about the American Revolution *is / are* really not how I want to spend my weekend.

3. The theory that seems to have most people confused about modern research in physics and astronomy *is / are* String Theory.

4. Practicing English every day, including the use of new vocabulary, *assist / assists* you in learning this language faster and better.

5. Few people, in my experience as an educator, really *appreciate / appreciates* the personal benefits of going back to school. Instead, they focus on their professional needs.

6. Corruption among the wealthiest members of developing nations *has / have* been cited as a chief cause of discontent and even revolution around the world.

7. The brightest lights in the night sky, which a large number of people *assume / assumes* to be stars, *is / are* in fact planets, in particular Venus and Jupiter.

8. The most popular shows that my family in Germany watch *come / comes* from the vast film industry of the United States, which always *generate / generates* new shows.

9. Reviewing decades of research on the health effects of smoking *has / have* finally pushed the government to take action and restrict where people *is / are* allowed to smoke.

10. A large amount of data *suggest / suggests* that most Americans still *do / does* not consistently follow the advice of health experts about diet and exercise.

11. What confuses me most about registration *is / are* what I am supposed to do after my name is put on a waiting list that *do / does* not even show me how many names are on the list.

ASTRONOMY   JOURNAL WRITING 6.2

Choose from the following options for your journal writing assignment:

1. So much astronomical research has been undertaken by men and women who possessed special skills and knowledge beyond simply what we think of as astronomy. Isaac Newton was a physicist and mathematician, as was Galileo, who was also a philosopher. Aristotle too was a philosopher, but he was also a biologist, naturalist, and linguist among many other things. The knowledge that we gain in diverse fields of study enhances how well we understand ourselves and the world around us. What would you argue are the most important subjects that people today should be required to study? Choose three to five subjects and explain why you think people should learn them.

2. Scientific investigation is clearly an ongoing process. Science is never finished. There is always more for us to learn, but there is also a great deal we thought we knew, but still have to re-examine. I am sure there are "facts" or "truths" that you have been expected to accept because these truths were declared by a religious or social leader, or these facts were promoted by scientists and educators. Have you ever learned that those people were wrong? Describe how this happened. What were you told to believe was true? How did you find out that it was actually wrong? Have you changed how slowly or quickly you learn and accept things because of these false facts, perhaps becoming more skeptical? What sources do you trust the most to provide you with reliable facts?

3. Astronomers have spent centuries studying what they can see in space using more and more elaborate tools and devices. Eventually, humans themselves began flying into space aboard spacecraft. In fact, we now live in an age in which tourist space travel is becoming possible. Is that something you would ever consider—traveling in space? Flying to distant planets? What do you think you will find there? Astronomers have long been open to the idea that there is life on other planets. What do you think alien life would be like? Can you describe them? How would they look? How would they behave? Would they be friendly? Or aggressive?

4. Scientific investigation proceeds—sometimes gradually, sometimes quickly—through a process of developing theories that serve to explain phenomena that we see in and around us. A theory may or may not in fact be true, but it has been tested, and through testing and experimentation, we hope that any given theory will be reliable—that we can depend on these theories to explain things and to help us take the next steps in research and learning. Newton presented his theory that gravity is a force, depending on mass, that not only holds us on the surface of the earth, but which also keeps the earth revolving around the sun. And he was right. As students, we are exposed to any number of theories to explain the planets, the sun, the moon, and us.

   a. Describe a theory that you have learned about. What does this theory say? How does it explain the world for you? Do you have any doubts about this theory? Do most people accept it as true?

   b. There are always more questions to ask about us and the world and the universe around us. Have you ever come up with your own explanations? Your own theories? Can you share how you have tried to understand or explain the world around you or how life works?

VOCABULARY LISTS for UNIT ONE: ARCHAEOLOGY			
word	**pronunciation**	**synonym**	**antonym**
attribute	ə TRI byūt		
demonstrate	DE mən strāt		
devote	de VŌT		
element	E lə mənt		
evidence	E vi dəns		
inevitably	i NE vi tə blē		
method	ME thəd		
persistent	pər SIS tənt		
region	RĒ gən		
research	RĒ sərch		
reveal	rə VĒL		
transformation	trans fər MĀ shən		
word	**pronunciation**	**synonym**	**antonym**
accumulation	ə cyū myə LĀ shən		
conduct	cən DUCT		
considerable	cən SI dər rə bəl		
contribution	con tri BYŪ shən		
crucial	CRŪ shəl		
document	DO cyə mənt		
duration	dər RĀ shən		
ensure	en SHUR		
illustrate	IL lə strāt		
indicate	IN di cāt		
so-called	SŌ called		
symbolic	sym BO lic		

VOCABULARY LISTS for UNIT TWO: LITERATURE			
word	**pronunciation**	**synonym**	**antonym**
absurd	əb SURD		
compose	cəm PŌS		
correspond	cōr rə SPOND		
despair	de SPĀR		
egotism	E gə ti zəm		
enlarge	en LARJ		
impressive	im PRES siv		
intricate	IN tri cat		
keen	kēn		
proposition	pro pə SI shən		
spectator	SPEC tā tər		
suffer	SUF fər		
word	**pronunciation**	**synonym**	**antonym**
ashamed	ə SHĀMD		
barren	BĀR rən		
comfort	COM fərt		
culminate	CUL mi nāt		
declare	de CLĀR		
demon	DĒ mən		
expose	eks SPŌZ		
senile	SĒ nīl		
torment	TŌR ment		
vision	VI zhən		
weep	wēp		
wicked	WI kəd		

VOCABULARY LISTS for UNIT THREE: MYTHOLOGY			
word	**pronunciation**	**synonym**	**antonym**
animated	A nə mā ted		
approach	ə PRŌCH		
aspect	AS spect		
assume	əs SŪM		
despite	des SPĪT		
eventually	e VEN tuəl lē		
fundamental	fən də MEN təl		
individual	in di VI du əl		
injury	IN jər rē		
obvious	OB vi əs		
possess	pəz ZES		
responsibility	re spons sə BI li tē		
word	**pronunciation**	**synonym**	**antonym**
achieve	ə CHĒV		
community	cə MŪ ni tē		
decline	de CLĪN		
derive	dər RĪV		
domain	dō MĀN		
dwell	dwel		
embrace	em BRĀS		
migration	mī GRĀ shən		
seize	sēz		
similar	SI məl lər		
task	task		
tragedy	TRA ge dē		

VOCABULARY LISTS for UNIT FOUR: POLITICAL SCIENCE			
word	**pronunciation**	**synonym**	**antonym**
apparently	ə PĀR rent lē		
authority	ə THŌR ri tē		
concept	CON cept		
exercise	EKS sər sīz		
function	FUNC shən		
institution	in sti TŪ shən		
perspective	pər SPEC tiv		
prohibit	prō HI bit		
reform	re FŌRM		
role	rōl		
significant	sig NI fi cənt		
tension	TEN shən		
word	**pronunciation**	**synonym**	**antonym**
administration	ad mi ni STRĀ shən		
category	CA tə gōr rē		
charter	CHAR tər		
colonist	CO lə nist		
discipline	DIS si plin		
essentially	es SEN təl lē		
establish	es STA blish		
participation	par tis si PĀ shən		
principle	PRIN si pəl		
restricted	re STRIC təd		
struggle	STRU gəl		
toleration	tol lər RĀ shən		

VOCABULARY LISTS for UNIT FIVE: BIOLOGY

word	pronunciation	synonym	antonym
compound	COM pound		
conclusion	cən CLŪ zhən		
distinct	dis STĒNCT		
evolution	e və LŪ shən		
identify	ī DEN ti fī		
microscopic	mī crə SCO pic		
occur	ə CUR		
organism	ŌR gə ni zəm		
perceive	pər CĒV		
prior	PRĪ ər		
sequence	SĒ qəns		
structure	STRUC shər		
word	**pronunciation**	**synonym**	**antonym**
analyze	A nə līz		
compel	cəm PEL		
constant	CON stənt		
emphasize	EM phə sīz		
interpretation	in tər prə TĀ shən		
observation	ob zər VĀ shən		
process	PROS ses		
promote	prə MŌT		
propose	prə PŌS		
scripture	SCRIP shər		
theory	THĒR ry		
variation	var rē Ā shən		

VOCABULARY LISTS for UNIT SIX: ASTRONOMY

word	pronunciation	synonym	antonym
appropriate	ə PRŌ prē at		
celestial	ce LES tē əl		
circumstance	CIR cəm stans		
detect	de TECT		
furthermore	FUR thər mōr		
omen	Ō men		
phenomenon	phe NO me non		
potential	pə TEN shəl		
precisely	pre CĪS lē		
predict	pre DICT		
specific	spe SI fic		
visible	VIZ zi bəl		
word	**pronunciation**	**synonym**	**antonym**
accelerate	aks SEL lər rāt		
approximately	ə PROKS si mət lē		
controversial	con tri VER shəl		
generate	GEN nər rāt		
hypothesis	hī PO the sis		
impose	im PŌZ		
period	PĒR rē əd		
rational	RA shən nəl		
relevant	REL lə vənt		
resolution	re sə LU shən		
revolution	re və LU shən		
velocity	və LO si tē		

CREDIT LINES

1. **Archaeology Unit:** Page 1: top: Image © Patricia Hofmeester, 2013. Used under license from Shutterstock, Inc.; bottom: Photo courtesy of George Ellington. Page 3: Image © Tischenko Irina, 2013. Used under license from Shutterstock, Inc. Page 4: top: Image © Lefteris Papaulakis, 2013. Used under license from Shutterstock, Inc.; bottom: Image © Netfalls - Remy Musser, 2013. Used under license from Shutterstock, Inc. Page 5: Photo courtesy of George Ellington. Page 6: Photo courtesy of George Ellington. Page 7: Photo courtesy of George Ellington. Page 11: Photo courtesy of George Ellington. Page 13: Image © Pressmaster, 2013. Used under license from Shutterstock, Inc. Page 14: Image © FineShine, 2013. Used under license from Shutterstock, Inc. Page 15: Image © Oscar Espinosa, 2013. Used under license from Shutterstock, Inc. Page 16: Image © Grigory Kubatyan, 2013. Used under license from Shutterstock, Inc. Page 21: 1) Image © sunsinger, 2013. Used under license from Shutterstock, Inc.; 2) Photo courtesy of George Ellington; 3) Image © Fedor Selivanov, 2013. Used under license from Shutterstock, Inc.; 4) Photo courtesy of George Ellington; 5) Image © Hung Chung Chih, 2013. Used under license from Shutterstock, Inc.; 6) Photo courtesy of George Ellington; 7) Photo courtesy of George Ellington.

2. **Literature Unit:** Page 25: Image © Everett Collection, 2013. Used under license from Shutterstock, Inc. Page 35: top: Image © Catalin Petolea, 2013. Used under license from Shutterstock, Inc.; bottom: Image © branislavpudar, 2013. Used under license from Shutterstock, Inc. Page 36: Image © Alicia Dauksis, 2013. Used under license from Shutterstock, Inc.

3. **Mythology Unit:** Page 45: 1) Photo courtesy of George Ellington; 2) Image © numforest, 2013. Used under license from Shutterstock, Inc.; 3) Photo courtesy of George Ellington; 4) Image © lrafael, 2013. Used under license from Shutterstock, Inc.; 5) Photo courtesy of George Ellington; 6) Image © Malgorzata Kistryn, 2013. Used under license from Shutterstock, Inc.; 7-9) Photos courtesy of George Ellington. Page 48: Image © Antonio Abrignani, 2013. Used under license from Shutterstock, Inc. Page 49: Image © Geoffrey Kuchera, 2013. Used under license from Shutterstock, Inc. Page 50: Image © Marques, 2013. Used under license from Shutterstock, Inc. Page 51: Image © McCarthy's PhotoWorks, 2013. Used under license from Shutterstock, Inc. Page 58: Image © Roger Hall, 2013. Used under license from Shutterstock, Inc. Page 59: Image © Pecold, 2013. Used under license from Shutterstock, Inc. Pagte 60: Image © NCG, 2013. Used under license from Shutterstock, Inc. Page 62: Image © Nick Lamb, 2013. Used under license from Shutterstock, Inc. Page 66: Image © Algol, 2013. Used under license from Shutterstock, Inc.

4. **Political Science Unit:** Page 70: Image © jsp, 2013. Used under license from Shutterstock, Inc. Page 71: Image © Netfalls - Remy Musser, 2013. Used under license from Shutterstock, Inc. Page 72: Image © Renata Sedmakova, 2013. Used under license from Shutterstock, Inc. Page 80: Image © spirit of america, 2013. Used under license from Shutterstock, Inc. Page 81: Image © Suchan, 2013. Used under license from Shutterstock, Inc.

5. **Biology Unit:** Page 88: Image © Matthew Cole, 2013. Used under license from Shutterstock, Inc. Page 91: top: Image © koya979, 2013. Used under license from Shutterstock, Inc.; bottom: Image © wavebreakmedia, 2013. Used under license from Shutterstock, Inc. Page 92: top: Image © ducu59us, 2013. Used under license from Shutterstock, Inc.; bottom: Image © Alila Medical Media, 2013. Used under license from Shutterstock, Inc. Page 93: Image © nobeastsofierce, 2013. Used under license from Shutterstock, Inc. Page 95: Image © Mopic, 2013. Used under license from Shutterstock, Inc. Page 102: Image © LeonP, 2013. Used under license from Shutterstock, Inc. Page 103: top: Image © Nicku, 2013. Used under license from Shutterstock, Inc.; bottom: Photo courtesy of George Ellington. Page 104: Image © Nicku, 2013. Used under license from Shutterstock, Inc. Page 105: Photo courtesy of George Ellington.

6. **Astronomy Unit:** Page 111: Image © Mopic , 2013. Used under license from Shutterstock, Inc. Page 114: top: Image © Neo Edmund, 2013. Used under license from Shutterstock, Inc.; bottom: Photo courtesy of George Ellington. Page 115: Image © Nataliya Hora, 2013. Used under license from Shutterstock, Inc. Page 116: top: Photo courtesy of George Ellington; bottom: Image © Avik, 2013. Used under license from Shutterstock, Inc. Page 122: Image © silver tiger, 2013. Used under license from Shutterstock, Inc. Page 125: Image © Nicku, 2013. Used under license from Shutterstock, Inc. Page 126: both: Image © Nicku, 2013. Used under license from Shutterstock, Inc. Page 127: top: Photo courtesy of George Ellington; bottom: Image © Nicku, 2013. Used under license from Shutterstock, Inc.

ENDNOTES

[1] As far as researchers can determine, the great Greek storyteller Homer probably lived around the 7th-8th centuries BC. And while he is typically referred to as the author of the two great Greek epics—*The Iliad* and *The Odyssey*—it is highly doubtful that Homer wrote these stories. It is more likely that he composed them and told them to audiences in the ancient Greek tradition of storytelling, and that others memorized his stories and continued telling them to audiences until at last they were written down by someone we simply do not know.

[2] Homer, *The Iliad,* trans. W. H. D. Rouse (New York: New American Library, 1962), 11.

[3] Ceram C.W., ed. *Hands on the Past* (New York: Alfred A. Knopf, 1966), 53.

[4] Silverberg R, *Great Adventures in Archaeology* (Lincoln: University of Nebraska Press, 1964), 313.

[5] Ibid., 343.

[6] Ibid., 373.

[7] There are other theories to explain the *tzolkin* calendar. For example, this calendar of 13 months may derive from the Mayan belief in 13 levels of the spiritual upperworld. There is even an idea that the *tzolkin* calendar was originally developed by Mayan midwives seeking a way of predicting the birth of a child, since a human pregnancy lasts around 260 days.

[8] Adapted from: Cushing F. H., *Zuni Folktales* 1901. Internet: Internet Sacred Text Archive. http://www.sacred-texts.com/nam/zuni/zft/index.htm Sep 2005.

[9] The diverse peoples identified in this text as Celts have been known by a number of different names over the last two millennia or so, reflecting not only the notions of the outside cultures who named them such, but also the fact that "Celt" is an umbrella term for many different cultures who have shared related languages. The ancient Greeks were the first outsiders to call these people Celts, as did the later Romans, who also referred to some Celtic peoples as Gauls. Most Celtic dialects are dead. Surviving dialects include Irish Gaelic, Scottish Gaelic, Welsh, Breton, Cornish, and Manx.

[10] The principle sources of information for this essay: Kagan D, *Pericles of Athens and the Birth of Democracy.* (New York: Free Press, 1991), and Barr S, *The Will of Zeus.* (New York: Dell Publishing, 1965).

[11] The only exception to this rule are mature red blood cells, which have neither a nucleus nor mitochondria, and therefore they are the only human cells to contain no DNA.

[12] A smaller amount of genetic information can also be found in mitochondrial DNA. In humans, all mitochondrial DNA stems from the mother, while DNA in the nucleus of the cell comes from both the mother and father.

[13] If you'd like to try, it would be approximately 58.66 times 10^{21} or 58.66 sextillion miles.

[14] Vedic Hinduism may be seen as an ancestral form of modern Hinduism. The name "Vedic" Hinduism derives from the "Vedas," which are the oldest known scriptural texts in Hinduism, composed around 2,500 to 3,500 years ago. Hindu tradition attributes these Vedic texts to Brahma, the Hindu god of creation.

[15] The law of gravity was not really understood until years later thanks to the research and observations of Galileo Galilei and Sir Isaac Newton.

[16] Isaac Newton proposed a *Universal Law of Gravity*, which essentially says that the gravitational pull of one object over another object can be calculated as the product of the masses of these two objects times a gravitational constant, which is then divided by the square of the distance between them. So for example, the gravitational pull of the earth on the moon is the mass of the earth times the mass of the moon times a gravitational constant divided by the distance between the earth and the moon squared. This means, of course, that the nearer the second object is to the first object, the stronger the gravitational pull.

CPSIA information can be obtained
at www.ICGtesting.com
Printed in the USA
BVHW010805250520
580268BV00006B/57